# THE MEANING OF
# ARCHAEOLOGY

## MASSIMO PALLOTTINO

*Professor of Etruscan Studies and Archaeology*
*The University of Rome*

## THAMES AND HUDSON · LONDON

TRANSLATED FROM THE ITALIAN
*Che cosa è l'Archeologia*
BY PEGGY MARTIN

# CONTENTS

So many books have appeared during the last few years on archaeology in general, its "adventures" and its discoveries, catering to the requirements of so many different types of reader, that to add yet another to their number might seem superfluous.

It must be said, however, that most of these books are essentially factual in character, dealing with the history of archaeological discoveries and the men who made them, or with fascinating aspects of ancient civilizations as revealed through their monuments. Only a very few works undertake the study of archaeological problems from the point of view of the methods, aims, and value of these investigations within the historical disciplines, and their effects on contemporary culture — or, in other words, attempt to take stock and consider possible future developments. And even these few, including, in recent years, valuable works by Sir Mortimer Wheeler, Grahame Clark, and J. A. H. Potratz, tend to lay the main emphasis on the handling of technical processes in archaeological research, of great interest at the present time, and reflect their authors' predilections for prehistoric antiquities, or those outside the classical world. This corresponds to a general reaction, which has taken place during the last ten years, against the centuries-old domination of classical studies and humanistic traditions, and an increasingly technical approach even in the field of investigations devoted to learning about the past.

I was therefore attracted to the idea of writing a brief new appraisal of the world of archaeology, taking into account all its manifestations, including its bearing on the needs and trends of present-day society — an aspect less frequently studied — and, of course, paying special attention to the most recent scientific developments; but at the same time trying to restore the balance of its fundamental historical and cultural value by pointing out the importance of the classical nucleus around which, when all is said and done, it has grown up in modern times.

This attempt to re-examine archaeological problems with the maximum objectivity and on as wide a front as possible, without any bias or prejudice, does nevertheless inevitably give a certain amount of special consideration to Italian experiences; this is justified not only by the fact that Italy was the cradle of antiquarian studies from the Renaissance to the beginning of the nineteenth century, but also because of the position occupied by that country at the present time in the field of international archaeological activities, particularly as regards certain departments of legislation, research techniques, museography, etc. This directly concerns the Italian public, of course; but it may also be of interest to the people of other countries. Moreover, the greatly increased output of archaeological literature at the present time includes hardly any Italian voices, and therefore some aspects of fundamental interest concerning the discovery and knowledge of the ancient world and its monuments have tended to be forgotten, seeing that all works of synthesis, however wisely impartial, are bound to reflect mainly the experiences, data, and examples most closely related to the author's nationality and field of activity.

But objectivity does not mean a lack of zeal and enthusiasm. The burning problems confronting archaeology throughout the world — the dangers threatening our archaeological patrimony, the vagueness of scientific direction, the lack of organization, etc. — are so many, and so serious, that they demand the attention and active intervention of scholars (who cannot remain absorbed in the sterile egoism of their private researches, but must assume every kind of responsibility in defense of the very objects of their studies). I have therefore not hesitated in these pages to single out and denounce the evils and errors which most preoccupy us at the present time, and to make appeals and suggestions for ways of remedying them.

Finally, since nowadays it is constantly reiterated that culture has a social function to perform, I would like to say that I have tried to present a picture of archaeology which will correspond with the widespread popular interest in this subject and will be easily understood by all — not only because of the point of view from which it is written, and the fascinating episodes it discusses, but also more especially because of the language used. I have deliberately avoided the difficult technical expressions which so often adorn the prose of the experts (as far as possible, that is, and adding explanatory notes where necessary). I hope that more knowledgeable readers will not hold this against me.

The numerous carefully selected illustrations follow the development of the text and provide visible examples in support of its argument. They are also intended to tell a story on their own, and could be "read" without the text; it was therefore considered important to supplement them with fairly full captions. Some of the subjects and many of the reproductions are published here for the first time. My thanks are due to my colleague Paola Zancani Montuoro, to Francesco Santi, Giuseppe Donato, the Istituto Centrale del Restauro, the Aerofototeca Nazionale, the Istituto Italiano di Paleontologia Umana, the Centro Sperimentale di Archeologia Sottomarina, the Laboratorio di Geologia Nucleare of Pisa University, and the Fondazione Lerici, for the photographs which they have kindly provided or brought to my notice.

This book owes its final form mainly to the co-operation of Orazio Pugliese, of the Casa Editrice Sansoni, who has devoted much care and enthusiasm to it, and Enzo Crea for the illustrations; my assistants Romolo Augusto Staccioli and Maria Teresa Falconi sought out illustrative material, revised proofs, and prepared indices; a number of photographs were made by Oscar Savio. To all these I wish to express my sincere gratitude.

MASSIMO PALLOTTINO

9

# THE MEANING OF ARCHAEOLOGY

Everyone is familiar with the evocative power of objects which once belonged to great men. No description or biography is capable of bringing us as close to their real image as a portrait, or the room in which they lived, the books, the instruments, the furniture which they handled. All these things can arouse curiosity and emotion even in those who are not in the habit of reading; they provide a direct contact with figures from the past. In other ages, relics of the saints were powerful stimulants for the piety of the masses, precisely because they were materially visible and tangible; we ourselves are moved with a special intensity when some memento of a dear one we have lost comes into our hands.

Tangible evidence stirs the imagination more deeply than memories and tradition, which require an effort of the mind; an antique object, or even one which is merely old, has an immediate, almost an intuitive fascination of its own. Fundamentally, the fascination of archaeology lies in this: in being able to cross a threshold trodden countless times by the contemporaries of Socrates or of Caesar; in holding for a moment a cup which, in effect, touched their lips; in seeing them represented on a relief or in a painting just as they were seen by the unknown artist of antiquity who made their image. Those stones, those objects, give forth mysterious emanations which seem to cause the intervening centuries to melt away.

Material remains and written tradition together provide the foundations on which the history of the past is reconstructed. Without the voice of tradition, history is like a silent landscape; but without material remains, it is like an echo of things described and related but never seen, lacking the flavor of direct experience. Memories are transmitted from mouth to mouth and from book to book through succeeding generations, subjected to all the wear and tear of time and all the changes made by the narrators; they make their appearance distorted by falsehood, errors, fanciful additions, the subjective interpretations of contemporaries or of those who followed later. On the other hand, the antique object — if it survives to our own time, and depending on its state of preservation — constitutes a definite, unaltered fact: a piece of evidence in the pure state. In this sense, archaeology provides a good vantage point from which to survey historical literature.

If we were to compare the reconstruction of the past with a large-scale police inquiry or a trial, tradition would be the equivalent of the depositions of the witnesses, and archaeological data would represent the material evidence: the former eloquent and circumstantial, but not always reliable; the latter fragmentary, not always clear in meaning, but in themselves incontrovertible. In the hunt for clues, in the ingenuity required to fit them into place, in the effort to interpret them logically, archaeologists do in fact very closely resemble criminal investigators. They operate on the front line of historical research like true detectives of the past. Perhaps this is why their work seems so exciting to the general public, who derive such enjoyment from reading detective stories or following the twists and turns of court cases.

Archaeologists, like detectives, are not content with studying clues already discovered, but are constantly in search of new ones, ever more numerous and significant. This determined approach is justified by the fact that, in the subsoil of lands where antique civilizations flourished, there are still hidden vast treasuries of buried evidence — sometimes just scratched on the surface by the excavator's pick, or as yet unknown and unpredictable. Here, too, archaeology differs from the study of historical records transmitted through literary sources. Except in rare cases, the historiographical patrimony is a known quantity, with definite limits and no longer capable of being augmented. The hope of discovering the lost books of Livy's history of Rome is a chimera no longer pursued by any but the occasional eccentric. Archaeological sources, on the other hand, are constantly providing new opportunities of increasing our knowledge through excavations.

Because of this, archaeologists have a special attitude toward the object of their studies, differing fundamentally from that of philologists, historians of ancient literatures, historians of law, and the like. These scholars are mainly concerned with commenting no and interpreting what is already known; archaeologists tend to search for the unknown. This brings us face to face with the second — and still more conspicuous — aspect of archaeological experience: that is to say, the feeling of continuous conquest, of the eager expectation and the joy of discovery. Moreover, these discoveries do not reveal a reality outside our own experience — like that of the cosmos, for example, to which natural scientists, physicists, and astronomers devote their researches. On the contrary, they bring to light something which directly concerns ourselves. To uncover little by little the road along which humanity has traveled in the past is a means of constantly increasing our understanding of our own human reality, its essential nature and its destiny. As Sir Mortimer Wheeler so tellingly puts it, we are excavating not "things" but human beings. The search, therefore, seems to us all the more thrilling and important.

It has been stated recently that archaeological research is not in itself a positive cultural factor unless it achieves critical results — in other words, the reconstruction of history. This is obviously true; and we shall have occasion to stress the point more than once, not only in connection with the romantic vision of archaeology as an "adventure," but even more with regard to its interpretation as a fashionable pastime or, still worse, a speculative activity. All the same, this very passion for research, this thirst for exploration regardless of the ends in view, is an important factor which corresponds to the modern world's restless desire to enlarge indefinitely all the frontiers of knowledge. In this sense, too, archaeology is part of the culture of our age, and even one of its most significant manifestations.

# A BRIEF HISTORY OF ARCHAEOLOGY

### The attitude of antiquity and the Middle Ages
### to the monuments of the past

For the peoples of antiquity, as for most civilizations earlier than that of the modern Western world or in any way outside it, the authority of tradition is of overwhelming importance. Truth is to be found, above all, in "what is written"; history is conceived as a collection of memories, either transmitted by word of mouth or enshrined in the works of ancient poets and storytellers. The Greek word "archaeologia" simply means ancient history.

The Greeks and Romans were doubtless aware of the mnemonic value of monuments bequeathed by previous generations. They admired the surviving works of famous artists, and delighted in strange objects recovered from the ground. Only in exceptional cases, however, did the idea come into their heads that these things could be used as direct and original sources of historical knowledge independent of literary tradition or even contradicting traditional accounts.

In antiquity, and from the time of the earliest civilizations of the Mediterranean world, such as that of the Egyptians, monuments which were erected with the deliberate intention of recording important events and personages (funerary stones, statues, buildings put up to honor or commemorate) were held in the same esteem as written records. They were regarded as true and genuine documents which could be bequeathed to posterity, though more conspicuous than the usual written records and of a more permanent character. Indeed, they almost always bore commemorative inscriptions and were themselves, therefore, an essential part of tradition. Horace, at the end of his third book of Odes (III, 30), boasts of having built a "monument" more lasting than bronze and higher than the Pyramids. Knowledge of the past was visualized as continuous and uninterrupted. All destruction involved the end of remembrance and

1. The Emperor Hadrian (reigned A.D. 117-38) was one of the great archaeologists of antiquity; he visited sites, collected works of art, and encouraged the artists of his time to adopt the classical style. Bust in the National Museum, Rome.

even, in a way, the annihilation of the past itself as a reality, whether such destruction were due simply to the passage of time or a deliberate action on the part of men (such as the *damnatio memoriae*, or defacement of monuments to those who had fallen into disfavor). Hence the constant effort to prevent tombs from falling into decay.

Nevertheless, in the field of art and culture there are occasional signs of a desire to imitate some particular period of the past, missing out intermediate phases and repudiating more recent traditions, with full awareness of a concept of interruption and resumption, and clearly drawing inspiration directly from monuments of the epoch chosen as a model. The famous passage from the elder Pliny (*Naturalis Historia*, XXXIV, 52), in which he states that art "came to an end" at the beginning of the third, and "revived anew" in the middle of the second century B.C., can be interpreted in this way. Evidently taste and criticism at the end of the Hellenistic period and in the early days of Imperial Rome rejected *en bloc* the naturalistic and "baroque" experiments of the Hellenistic world and turned back to the formal ideals of the classical art of the fifth and fourth centuries B.C., attempting to imitate and revive it. This reflex cultural movement had its intellectual origins in Athens (Pliny's source

2. Hadrian erected an Egyptian obelisk on the Pincian Hill in Rome in memory of his favorite, Antinoüs. This detail shows a portion of the west side, and in the right-hand strip the word Rome is written in hieroglyphs.

ON PAGES 20-21

3. View of Hadrian's Villa near Tivoli. Here the Emperor reconstructed some of the famous monuments he had admired in Greece and in the East, including the Lyceum, the Academy, the Prytaneum, and the Poikile at Athens (the latter can be seen in the foreground), the Vale of Tempe in Thessaly (left), and the Canopus Canal near Alexandria in Egypt (right).

is probably the Athenian critic Apollodorus), but reached its fullest development in Rome, where, particularly during the reigns of Augustus and his successors, we can see the spread of a classicizing fashion which looks back directly to the past, copying and elaborating on Greek sculpture and painting of the "golden age," often recasting and blending together its designs, and even drawing inspiration from archaic works appreciated only for their "antique" style without any reference to tradition, with an enjoyment which can be truly described as archaeological.

The chance discoveries of relics from past epochs — which were frequent, of course, where the lives of so many generations had succeeded one another in the same place — or the deliberate search for such things sometimes acquired the value of a cultural activity, beyond that of a mere episodic occurrence. We have considerable evidence of tombs being broken into for the sake of their valuable contents, particularly anything made of gold. This was a very widespread practice, and regarded by the ancients themselves as sacrilege. But there were times when purely material considerations were intermingled with the interests of the collector; in other words, certain finds took on a special value by virtue of their being works of art, or

4. King Ludwig the Bavarian's seal, showing some of the ancient monuments still standing in medieval Rome. Among them, on the left bank of the Tiber (from top to bottom): the Pyramid of Gaius Cestius, the Colosseum, a triumphal arch, the Column of Marcus Aurelius, the Pantheon; on the right bank, the obelisk of Nero's Circus close to the Vatican Basilica, and the Castel Sant'Angelo (the tomb of Hadrian). 1328. National Archives, Munich.

because of their rarity, or simply because they were "antiques." This implies a cultural attitude proper to a particular period or a particular society. It is not without reason that, when the classicizing and archaizing fashion mentioned above was at its height, the archaeological discoveries made by Caesar's veterans when they were rebuilding the old Greek city of Corinth caused such a stir in cultivated Roman society. The latter took to purchasing for very large sums the vases and bronzes brought to light when the old tombs were rifled (hence the prevalent use of the term *nekrokorinthia* for these objects), until the supply was exhausted, as Strabo relates (*Geography*, VIII, 6, 23).

There are other examples of even greater interest. During the purification of the sanctuary of Delos in 426 B.C., several tombs came to light; the historian Thucydides, who was present at the excavations and examined the finds, especially weapons, interpreted them as "evidence" of the presence of Carian peoples in the Aegean islands in very early times (Thucydides, I, 8, 1). For the first time, in other words, we find archaeological data used for the purpose of historical reasoning. Topographical investigations, the reconnaissance of ancient monuments, the reading of inscriptions on tombs, and the gathering of information about characters from the past formed part of the methods of study of scholarly Romans such as the elder Cato or the learned Varro, and also, probably, of the Greek historians of the Hellenistic period. Cicero recalls having sought and discovered, near Syracuse, the long-lost tomb of Archimedes, recognizing its characteristics and the text of the inscription (*Tuscalanae Disputationes*, V, 25).

This vein of observant erudition continued from antiquity into the culture of the Middle Ages, permeating Byzantium and even the Arab world. Here and there we find glimpses of it reflected in descriptions of antique monuments and inscriptions. But it becomes more and more tenuous as society changes, together with its ideals. The sense of history grows weaker, and a knowledge of the past tends to be restricted within the narrow confines of a few literary traditions — and even those are secondhand. The medieval mentality is on the whole one of complete confidence in tradition, in the authority of the *ipse dixit*, and in the value of preconstituted ideas and notions. The attitude to material relics of the past, to monuments, can therefore only be of a practical or ideological nature. Such things are restored, patched up, made use of if necessary, or else destroyed as a sign of paganism or idolatry; never, or hardly ever, are they considered from the point of view of their historical or documentary significance, or studied objectively with this in mind. Even in the case of early Christian monuments, the memorials of the martyrs, direct observation is lacking; instead, any information about their discovery is wrapped up in a complicated tissue of more or less apocryphal stories and legends.

Of course, Rome continued to exert an enormous influence, with all her splendors both sacred and profane, and the imposing mass of her great ancient buildings, then in a much better state of preservation than they are now, and which one could not fail to see and admire. We hear echoes of this admiration in the accounts left by pilgrims. It inspired a curious medieval work, the *Mirabilia Urbis Romae* (*The Marvels of Rome*), of which numerous versions and amplifications are extant. It does not, however, involve a genuine interest in study, much less research, and we find the *Mirabilia* padded out with fragments of early topographical writings such as the late-empire "Regionari," with pseudo-historical scraps of information, and with Biblical and mythological allusions; it suggests very odd origins and names for some of the ancient monuments, calling the Theater of Marcellus the "Basilica of Jupiter," the Pyramid of Gaius Cestius the "Tomb of Remus," etc.

ON PAGE 24

*5, 6. Above, detail of a Roman sarcophagus with Phaedra and Hippolytus, now in the Camposanto, Pisa. Below, Nativity by Nicola Pisano from the Marble Pulpit, Baptistery, Pisa. 1259-60. The Nativity shows the classical influence exerted by such monuments as the sarcophagus upon the art of the " first Renaissance " in thirteenth-century Italy.*

## The Renaissance and the rediscovery of "antiquity"

The humanistic awakening approached the knowledge of the classical world in an entirely new spirit — a desire to recapture the thought and ideals of the ancients in their true essence, no longer on a foun-

COLORPLATE I. *Painted wall decoration in the Domus Aurea (Golden House) of Nero, Rome.*

7. *One of the bronze tablets unearthed at Gubbio in 1456. Its sacred inscriptions are in Umbrian dialect, and the alphabet is a mixture of Umbrian and Latin. Palazzo dei Consoli, Gubbio.*

dation of uncertain traditions, but through the direct study of literary works and actual monuments.

In the beginning, the literary side of humanism is dominant. Texts are salvaged, read, annotated; the history and institutions of antiquity are reconstructed, using the Latin writers as the main source and deriving inspiration from them as models. But even in Petrarch's time the recollection of Rome's greatness, with its dreams of a rebirth, was already drawing additional nourishment from the influence of that city's noble ruins, and from sculpture, inscriptions, and antique coins. Imbued with such a spirit, Cola di Rienzo illumined his brief and tragic political venture with the enthusiasm of the archaeologist: "Every day he meditated upon the marble carvings which lay around Rome... only he could read the ancient inscriptions... he correctly interpreted those marble figures," as his chronicler relates. The description of Roman monuments, amplifying the account contained in the medieval *Mirabilia* by means of ever wider and more accurate observation, became a favorite literary genre among humanists of the fourteenth and fifteenth centuries — from Cola di Rienzo himself to Poggio Bracciolini, from Flavio Biondo to Pomponio Leto, from Leon Battista Alberti to the *Hypnerotomachia Poliphili* of Francesco Colonna, culminating in the great topographical treatises of the sixteenth century, such as those of Andrea Fulvio, Lucio Fauno, Bartolomeo Marliani, and Pirro Ligorio. The Roman antiquarians even had a society of their own, a sort of academy with its headquarters on the Quirinale, founded in 1478 by Pomponio Leto and flourishing for several decades.

But a more lively and genuine archaeological curiosity, as we now understand the expression, seems to manifest itself outside this circle of scholarly activity. The first to embark on actual excavations among the ruins of Rome were, in fact, two Florentine artists, Filippo Brunelleschi and Donatello. Architects and sculptors did not only seek an ideal symbol in the tangible evidence of the classical world; they were also looking more especially for a direct source of inspiration for their creative energy. They were able, therefore, to study antique remains in their actuality, appraising them with the concreteness of technicians, measuring buildings and reproducing figures. So, too, the first direct knowledge of Greek and Oriental antiquity is due, not to formal scholarship, but to the initiative and spirit of observation of a merchant from Ancona, Ciriaco de' Pizzicolli (1391–1455), who, during his many long journeys in those regions, tirelessly collected information and objects, copied inscriptions, described monuments and made drawings of them.

In the climate of humanism, therefore, but in circumstances and with aspects and aims differing from those of literary humanism, there was born a new interest in antiquities and the search for them. Attention was concentrated on archaeological discoveries, hitherto neglected; many of these enjoyed popular acclaim as great events, exciting the enthusiasm of scholars and artists, and contributing in

8. *In every age the Colosseum has been the most important symbol of the ancient glory of Rome. But the Renaissance architects it inspired utilized it as a stone quarry. The detail shows (from bottom to top) the three orders: Tuscan, Ionic, and Corinthian.*

9-11. *Antique models reflected in the architectural ideals of the humanists: above left, the Tempio Malatestiano at Rimini, by Leon Battista Alberti; above right, shell-decorated cupola on the tribune apse of Florence Cathedral, by Filippo Brunelleschi; below, view of an ideal town by an unknown artist. Second half of the fifteenth century. Ducal Palace, Urbino.*

12. Ever since the Renaissance the Apollo Belvedere, discovered in the fifteenth century and now in the Vatican Museum, has been one of the most famous and revered statues of antiquity. Inspired by classical models of the fourth century B.C., it belongs to the late Hellenistic period. Today it seems rather cold and self-conscious.

13. A Renaissance artist admiring the antique—the Apollo Belvedere on the left and the Laocoön group on the right. This drawing by Taddeo Zuccari is in the Department of Prints, Uffizi Gallery, Florence.

14. The Laocoön, discovered in 1506, was for centuries the most famous statue of classical antiquity. Probably dating from the second century B.C., it is the work of Agesander, Athenodorus, and Polydorus of Rhodes. Today it is in the Belvedere Courtyard of the Vatican Museum. The illustration shows the traditional restoration of Montorsoli, which has now been replaced by that of Filippo Magi.

32

no small measure to the development of contemporary culture. In 1485, a sarcophagus containing the almost intact body of a young girl was discovered on the Appian Way; it was exhibited at the Campidoglio, where it evoked the astonished admiration of the public. In 1489, a tomb was found near Corneto — in the necropolis of ancient Tarquinii — probably intact, and full of objects made of gold. In 1493, beneath the Esquiline Hill in Rome, the rooms of the Domus Aurea, Nero's fabulous Golden House, were laid open and visited; their fresco decorations are still among the most magnificent and most elegant of all the surviving painting of antiquity, and under the name *grottesche* (grotesques), derived from the "grottoes" where they were discovered, were a major source of inspiration for the decorative painting of the Renaissance, particularly Raphael's Vatican Loggias. In 1506, the marble group of the Laocoön came to light, in the same area as the Domus Aurea; admired and restored by Michelangelo, it became, along with the Apollo Belvedere, the most famous piece of sculpture of classical antiquity. Discoveries continued to be made during the sixteenth century, at increasingly frequent intervals and with mounting excitement: the statue of the Nile, the Farnese Bull, the Children of Niobe, the tomb of the Empress Maria, wife of Honorius, with all its precious furnishings, the first catacombs, Hadrian's Villa near Tivoli, the bronze Chimera from Arezzo (restored by Benvenuto Cellini).

In addition, systematic archaeological excavations were begun, with precise objectives and at considerable expense; these were undertaken not only in order to discover works of art but also to obtain information about the architecture and topography of ancient Rome. In these undertakings the Farnese family, who dominated the cultural life of Rome in the middle decades of the sixteenth century, were particularly distinguished for their munificence. Attention was concentrated upon the Baths of Caracalla and the Forum. The topographer Pirro Ligorio, who worked in Rome and at Hadrian's Villa near Tivoli, can be regarded as the first "militant" archaeologist to have achieved fame and enjoyed an official position; but even at the beginning of the century, when more and more discoveries were being made and the monuments of antiquity were arousing increased interest, Pope Leo X had appointed Raphael as official in charge of the antiquities of Rome.

There is no doubt that during the Renaissance archaeological research received a powerful stimulus not only from the enthusiasm for antique art, but also from the collecting mania. This phenomenon will be dealt with more specifically in a later chapter. But it is clearly impossible to present a satisfactory picture of antiquarian culture in Rome during the fifteenth and sixteenth centuries — in fact, it would be incomprehensible — without pointing out that by 1471 Sixtus IV had already assembled a number of famous pieces of sculpture (some of them from the Lateran) in the Palazzo del Campidoglio, including the Capitoline Wolf and the Spinario; that many Italian princes and

COLORPLATE II. *This Chimera from Arezzo represents the first encounter of the modern Renaissance world with Etruscan civilization. It was discovered in 1553 and restored by Benvenuto Cellini. Today it is in the Archaeological Museum in Florence. Made of bronze, it was probably part of a votive group dating from the fifth century* B.C.

15. *The relics of antiquity were much alive in the popular mind of papal Rome. The "Pasquino" was discovered at the beginning of the sixteenth century. It is a replica of a Hellenistic group of Menelaus and Patroclus, and was for centuries the personification of Roman political satire, the so-called pasquinade.*

rulers of the fifteenth century — the Aragonese in Naples, Lorenzo de' Medici in Florence, and the Gonzaga in Mantua, for example — had established the nucleus of a collection of antiquities at their courts; that Pope Julius II created the Belvedere Museum in the Vatican in 1506; and that the great collections built up by the Roman cardinals (Medici, Chigi, Della Valle, and above all Farnese) were initiated immediately afterwards (the Farnese collection grew into the biggest museum of antique sculpture in the sixteenth century). This enthusiasm and pride, coupled with patronage of the arts and of letters, soon spread throughout Italy, particularly Florence and Venice, into France at the court of Francis I, and into the palaces of the German princes at Munich, Vienna, and Dresden.

As far as a love of classical works of art is concerned, we may find it rather hard nowadays to understand the attitude of the men of the Renaissance with regard to the fate of antique architectural monuments. The period under discussion was responsible for more deliberate destruction than occurred throughout all the medieval centuries: the Colosseum was ransacked to provide building materials for Pius II (who had been the highly cultivated humanist Aeneas Silvius Piccolomini); the old Byzantine basilica of St. Peter's was demolished without scruple or regret, resulting in the loss of countless treasures of late antique art; stone for the fabric of the new basilica was drawn from all the monuments of Rome, particularly the Forum and the Baths of Caracalla; the town planning of Sixtus V and the

16-18. *Original documents of the plan to preserve the ancient Porta Marzia in the new bastion of the fortress built by Antonio da Sangallo for Pope Paul III at Perugia (1540-43). In the lower drawing, Sangallo has written above the door: "I want the whole of the ancient arch and both the pilasters to be seen, and I want the new wall to be as shown by the pen strokes." Above, detail of another drawing showing the sculptural decoration of the gate. Department of Prints, Uffizi Gallery, Florence. Opposite, a present-day view of the Porta Marzia.*

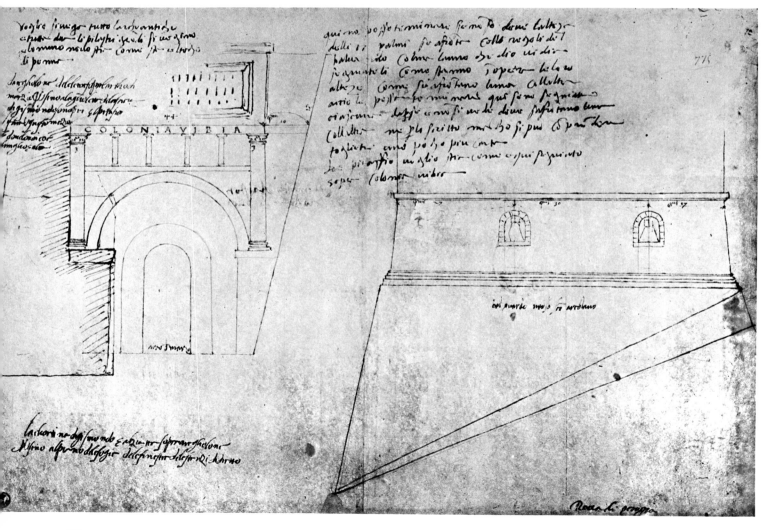

alignment of the streets wrought havoc with such buildings as the Baths of Diocletian and the Septizonium of Septimius Severus. To set against this powerful constructive urge with its resultant vandalism (typical of the dual spirit of the Renaissance — looking back to antiquity yet reaching forward to the modern world), we find, nevertheless, examples of enlightened regard. Sangallo, for instance, incorporated the façade of the old Porta Marzia into the bastions of his Rocca Paolina at Perugia, whilst Paul III issued a papal bull requiring that protective measures be taken. There were acts of protest like that of the Roman officials who opposed Sixtus V and, supported by the prudent vacillations of the architect Domenico Fontana, managed at the last minute to save from destruction the tomb of Cecilia Metella and the arch of Janus al Velabro. The cult of antiquity was no longer confined to scholarly circles and the palaces of rich patrons.

To the men of the Italian Renaissance, this cult was essentially an appeal to the memory of their forefathers, a return to the great days of Rome. Research and inquiry were entirely directed to the rediscovery of what had been lost or hidden during the "barbarian" centuries, in order to bring back to life its ideals and forms. Rome, in fact, remained almost the only object and theater of study.

## The learned antiquarianism of the courts and academies

The Renaissance attitude toward the antique seems to have been inherited by the age of Baroque, and to have manifested itself in the same way. Archaeological discoveries, particularly of sculpture, continued to arouse excitement and stimulate studies; more collections were formed by cardinals and princes (Ludovisi, Barberini, etc.); interest in Roman topography resulted in the production of such monumental works as those of Pier Sante Bartoli and Gian Pietro Bellori. At the same time, however, the pickax destroyed the Temple of Minerva in the Forum of Nerva, the Arch of Portogallo, and the Basilica of Junius Bassus; and Urban VIII had the dome of the Pantheon stripped of its bronze covering (whence the famous epigram coupling Barberini with barbarians — *Quod non fecerunt barbari, fecerunt Barbarini*). Contemporary art and letters continued to draw inspiration from classical mythology and ancient Rome.

However, if we compare seventeenth-century culture with the "golden age" of the Renaissance, it becomes clear that the lively, spontaneous urge, rich in idealistic content, which in the fifteenth and early sixteenth centuries had stimulated all sorts of people — scholars, artists, statesmen, private individuals — to admire ancient monuments and to search for antiquities, tended gradually to weaken and change

*19-21. Above left, portrait of the abbot Luigi Lanzi. Engraving by G. Masselli from Onofrio Boni,* In Praise of Don Luigi Lanzi. *Above right, portrait in oil of Johann Joachim Winckelmann, by A. Maron. 1768. Schlossmuseum, Weimar. Below, discovery of the Temple of Isis at Pompeii. Print by P. Fabris.*

into a fashionable pursuit of scholars, men of letters, and high society. Moreover, the problems of the religious struggles, the establishment of the great European monarchies, and the new directions taken by the arts and sciences, seemed to be guiding society toward other interests in which classicism was reabsorbed, overpowered, or even denied.

The collecting of antiquities and the undertaking of archaeological researches, initiated by the wealthy Renaissance patrons, seem in the century of absolutism to have been drawn more and more into the sphere of the sovereign's magnificence and cultural paternalism. The most famous example of an excavation undertaken for reasons of dynastic glory is that of Herculaneum and Pompeii, the two cities buried by the eruption of Vesuvius in A.D. 79, whose archaeological treasures were revealed toward the middle of the eighteenth century at the behest of the Bourbons of Naples. The objects recovered from these sites were collected together to form, first at Portici and later (after 1822) in Naples, what is still one of the greatest museums of antiquities in the whole world. Likewise, France under Louis XIV undertook important work in connection with the discovery of ancient monuments in the Hellenistic East.

The study of antiquity, having lost the ardor of humanistic ideals, turns into a preoccupation with minute details, a pastime of the erudite world, almost a parlor game. The figure of the learned cleric is born — full of miscellaneous learning, but also a keen and patient observer who spends his whole life collecting and studying carvings and inscriptions. Bernard de Montfaucon (1655–1741) was a man of this kind; he left behind a vast work in ten volumes on every aspect of the peoples of antiquity as seen through their monuments. Scholars enjoyed meeting together to hold discussions, sometimes to oppose one another in bitter controversies; academies flourished, with all their attendant pomp and ceremony. In 1665 Louis XIV founded the Académie des Inscriptions et Belles Lettres; in 1727 the Etruscan Academy of Cortona was instituted; in 1740 Benedict XIV created the Roman Accademia di antichità profane (later changed to the Accademia Pontificia Romana di Archeologia); in 1755 the Reale Accademia Ercolanese was formed in Naples; while the Anglo-Saxon world showed from then on its preference for private associations with the foundation in London, in 1733, of the Society of Dilettanti.

The antiquarian studies of the seventeenth and eighteenth centuries showed a certain tendency to specialize, characteristic of their period and in opposition to the universality of humanism. It manifested itself in the frequency of works devoted solely to painting, to portraits, to coins, to inscriptions. These works often had the character of systematic collections. The very detachment of classical scholarship from the more living problems of contemporary thought and culture, and its tendency to become an end in itself (and not a means of rediscovering the past), constituted in a sense a positive factor paving the way for a more scientific attitude. Furthermore, the sphere of historico-archaeological interests tended to broaden, spreading beyond the confines of Rome and Roman antiquities, even beyond the Graeco-Roman civilization, to embrace the study of exotic or local antiquities. This is illustrated by the speculations of the Jesuit Athanasius Kircher (1602–1680), founder of the Collegio Romano museum (the Kircheriano), on Egyptian monuments and hieroglyphics; the impetus given to study and research in connection with Etruscan antiquities, particularly in Tuscany, by the publication of the work by the Scotsman T. Dempster and with the encouragement of the Academy of Cortona (giving rise to a fashion half-jokingly christened *etruscheria*); the discovery in 1654 of the tomb of the Frankish king Childeric I at Tournai, which had widespread repercussions. European culture had, however, already come into direct and lasting contact, during the seventeenth century, with the monuments of ancient Greece, through the travels, accounts, and investigations of the Frenchmen Louis de Hayes, Jacob Spon, and above all Charles-François Olier, Marquis of Nointel and Louis XIV's ambassador to the Sultan's court. During the eighteenth century there was continued and widespread activity in Asia Minor and Syria, particularly on the part of English amateurs.

But about halfway through the eighteenth century, a powerful impulse toward a new classical renaissance began to make itself felt in Rome, in the field of scholarship as well as in the arts and in taste. It germinated in the circle of Cardinal Alessandro Albani, and its most ardent supporter was Johann Joachim Winckelmann, founder of the history of classical art. In contrast to the erudition of the period immediately preceding it, this movement took on a distinctly ideological character. Contemporary society set out to model itself on antiquity; the French Revolution and the Napoleonic Empire breathed its atmosphere. European Neoclassical art was born. Clearly this acted as a powerful new driving force for Graeco-Roman archaeology. Fresh excavations were carried on in and around Rome, other parts of Italy, and elsewhere; antique works of art were praised and collected (Napoleon himself treated them as precious spoils of war); great new museums were established (the Vatican Museum, the Louvre, the Munich Pinakothek); above all, antiquity and classical art were studied with renewed energy, not only by Winckelmann but by such distinguished men as Ennio Quirino Visconti, Carlo Fea, and Antonio Nibby.

At the height of the Neoclassical enthusiasm, the English ambassador to Constantinople, Lord Elgin (Thomas Bruce), managed to remove from the temples on the Acropolis in Athens the marble sculptures which constituted the noblest testimony to classical Greek art of the golden age of Phidias. Like the discovery of the Laocoön at the beginning of the sixteenth century, the revelation to the world of the Elgin Marbles marked the point of departure for a new phase in the knowledge of the ancient world — and, in a broader sense, in the development of European culture.

22, 23. *Above, the interior of the Great Pyramid, Giza. Below, the Sphinx, Giza. Illustrations from J.-F. Champollion,* Monuments de l'Égypte et de la Nubie . . .

### The great romantic adventure

If we compare the learned men engaged in classifying antique objects during the seventeenth and eighteenth centuries with those restless travelers who, in the same period, explored all the pathways of the Mediterranean Orient, crossing seas and deserts in search of ruins of the remote past, we see how different are the forms taken, even in those days, by the passion for archaeology.

At the Battle of the Pyramids, Napoleon had assembled the frightened scientists accompanying his expedition in the positions of

24, 25. Above, the amphitheater at Pompeii at the beginning of the nineteenth century. From a contemporary print. Below, painted tomb at Tarquinii, discovered at the end of the eighteenth century. From James Byres, Hypogaei or Sepulchral Caverns of Tarquinia, 1872.

greatest safety, at the center of his squares — along with the donkeys, according to the unkind remark attributed to him. Yet a very few years later Giovanni Battista Belzoni of Padua, with an unquenchable thirst for adventure, had boldly entered the awe-inspiring Egyptian funerary chambers alone. Ascending the Nile through Nubia, he discovered the colossal rock temple of Abu Simbel (which is still one of the wonders of the world, and which civilized humanity went to great lengths to save from being drowned in the waters of the Nile when the new Aswan Dam was built), and he penetrated into the desert as far as the legendary Oasis of Amon.

Romantic archaeology was born in the East. It fed upon a sense of mystery. It pondered on the impermanence of all human things (so tellingly expressed in a few lines in Shelley's *Ozymandias*) and indulged in dreams of discovering unknown marvels, far removed from a familiar, almost a living past like that of the classical world. In Europe, this Romantic archaeology came unexpectedly, at the beginning of the nineteenth century, upon a strange, unforeseeable field for development in Etruria. A few miles away, Rome still lived in the classicizing dream of an antiquity of sculpture and architecture — the dream of Winckelmann and Visconti, of Bertel Thorvaldsen and Antonio Canova — when suddenly the marshland of Latium and Tuscany disclosed its treasures. Myriad painted vases were unearthed at Vulci; frescoes depicting scenes full of life were discovered on the walls of the tombs of Tarquinii; Cerveteri revealed the barbaric splendor of its gold objects, fashioned in an Oriental style. Color, movement, exotic forms, the appearances of a flesh-and-blood reality, rose up in opposition to the pale marble figures, the idealization of academic canons of perfection. The archaeological passion left the cool twilight of the Neoclassical museums and emerged into the sun, the wild thickets, the rocky countryside.

26-28. *Discoveries of the Etruscan burial places. Left, the interior of the Tomb of the Merchants at Tarquinii. From James Byres,* Hypogaei or Sepulchral Caverns of Tarquinia, *1872. Above, the name Bonap[arte] with other traces of modern writing recently observed on the wall of an Etruscan tomb at Vulci. Lucien Bonaparte, who became Prince of Canino, ransacked the necropolis at Vulci, carrying out intensive excavations between 1828 and 1840. Below, interior of the Alcove Tomb at Cerveteri discovered in 1845.*

29. *The removal of the Parthenon frieze to London (1803-12) by Lord Elgin marks the direct encounter of European culture with classical Greek art. Detail of Athenian horsemen on the north frieze, designed and executed by Phidias. c. 440 B.C. British Museum.*

48

*30. Tower "H" and the eastern part of the city wall with the "S" gate on the Acropolis at Troy (Level VI, 1800-1300 B.C., middle and late bronze age).*

*31. Sophia Schliemann wearing the so-called Treasure of Priam. From* Atlas Trojanischer Alterthümer . . . von Dr. Heinrich Schliemann.

The initiative passed out of the hands of court antiquarians into those of enthusiastic explorers and rough tomb searchers. Erudition was transformed into adventure.

It is easy to imagine that the Romantic approach to archaeology may have been more congenial to the Nordic spirit, and may have found inspiration in Novalis' dreamy mysticism, or Hölderlin's spirit of Dionysiac expansion toward distant worlds. It is certainly a fact that the first impetus was given to the resurrection of Etruria by a group of German scholars and amateurs who had met in Rome in about 1820 and had formed a circle known as the Hyperboreans — E. Gerhard, A. Kestner, and Baron O. von Stackelberg. These men were soon joined by a varied and picturesque assortment of investigators: personalities like Lucien Bonaparte, the youngest and least conformist of Napoleon's brothers, who had become Prince of Canino and a country gentleman, and who discovered the necropolis of Vulci; financiers like G. P. Campana, who, after devastating half Etruria with his excavations and building up an enormous collection, was involved in the bankruptcy of the Monte di Pietà in Rome (a money-lending establishment, founded in the seventeenth century, of which he was director) and ended up in prison; local *dilettanti* like C. Avvolta, *gonfalionere* or standard-bearer of Corneto and an indefatigable excavator of tombs; as well as landowners, priests, country people, and laborers who live again, as in a kaleidoscope, in George Dennis' famous book on the Etruscan cities and burial grounds.

At the same time, the active salvaging of Greek works of art and the very classicism of European official circles seemed themselves to be in tune with the impassioned and heroic themes of the period, and to be permeated with the influence of German minds. The Romantic epic of the liberation of Greece from Turkish dominion had unfolded in an atmosphere of re-evocation of that country's ancient

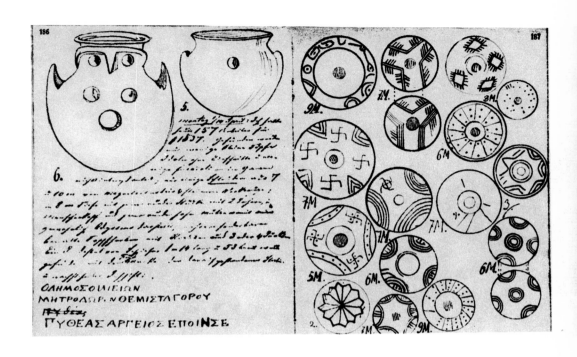

32. *Two pages from one of Heinrich Schliemann's diaries, relating to the excavations at Troy.*

glories. The Bavaria of Ludwig I, an ardent admirer and collector of Greek works of art, provided Greece with a sovereign (Prince Otto) and, along with him, technicians, architects, and archaeologists. Philhellenism was both a political attitude and an archaeological passion; thenceforward, an indissoluble intellectual bond was formed between Hellenism and Germanism. Furthermore, the Frenchman Champollion, the Tuscan Rosellini, and the German Lepsius restored a countenance and a tongue to ancient Egypt. The Piedmontese Botta and the Englishman Layard disinterred the ruins of Assyria, while another Englishman, the traveler and dilettante Charles Fellows, explored Asia Minor, discovering, publicizing, and pillaging its monuments. Almost everywhere, the activity of the archaeologist was preceded by that of the adventurer — or the adventurer himself became the archaeologist.

Finally, when the Greek and Turkish Levant had already become one vast excavation, in an age which was to turn from dreams to the positive conquests of science, there appeared the last and greatest of the Romantic archaeologists — Heinrich Schliemann. He, too, was a Northerner, a native of Mecklenburg. A businessman, he had been imbued from infancy with classical ideals, and was a devoted reader of Homer. With sublime simplicity, he set himself the task of resurrecting from the earth the heroes of the Greek epic. In 1871, he drove his pick into the hill of Hissarlik in Asia Minor — and uncovered the walls and treasures of Troy. Three years later, he began to excavate at Mycenae, in the actual kingdom of the Atridae. As if by magic, there came to light fantastic tombs gleaming with gold, which he attributed unhesitatingly to the characters of the *Iliad*. A whole world of new marvels opened out before the eyes of astounded and mystified scholars. Greek history leapt back a further thousand years into the past, because of the incredible intuitive genius of one man.

## Modern scientific archaeology

In the course of the nineteenth century, archaeology became a science. It acquired full awareness of its own nature and objectives, with the establishment of the experimental method also applied to historical studies. Nowadays, in fact, antique monuments and remains tend to free themselves from the influence of humanistic ideals and to become more than individual curiosities, acquiring instead the value of positive data, of material and objective "proofs" with which to reconstruct past history. The importance of archaeology, as an autonomous discipline, has gone on increasing progressively, while the traditional sources — in other words, the works of the classical authors — seem to be more and more questioned by modern critical opinion.

In connection with these new requirements, however, it was necessary for archaeological data to be collected, studied, classified, and interpreted systematically and objectively. Any casual elements remaining in the search for such data had to be eliminated; there was to be no lack of clarity in their description, no emotion or caprice in their interpretation.

Exploration and excavation could no longer be left, as hitherto, to the discretion of amateurs, rich patrons, or adventurers. These activities had to be disciplined in a program of systematic work carried out in accordance with precise scientific directives. Publication of new finds became a technical necessity, instead of a literary diversion; it became a question of presenting dispassionately the true characteristics of ancient monuments and objects, with regard to both their form and the context in which they were found. For this reason photography, as a means of faithful mechanical reproduction, quickly replaced sketches, drawings, and engravings, becoming the universal and indispensable ally of archaeology which it is today. Antiquarian and mythological disquisitions have been replaced by the search for comparisons, the concrete study of types, styles, and chronology; erudition and improvisation have yielded to scientific rationality.

But it went further than that. Until the beginning of the nineteenth century the archaeologist had been essentially a solitary worker — a humanist or a dilettante. As the technical experiments and ideas of modern archaeology grew more firmly established and more widely known, it gradually became evident that there was a need for "professional" bodies. Scientific co-operation and the organization of labor had become essential. A system of training was indispensable; archaeology became a part of the teaching program of the universities. Specialized libraries were formed. The various academies were replaced by societies and institutes established as centers for collective work. (The prototype of these new organizations was the Istituto di Corrispondenza Archeologica, founded in Rome in 1829.) Individual researches have given way to organized expeditions, in which

53

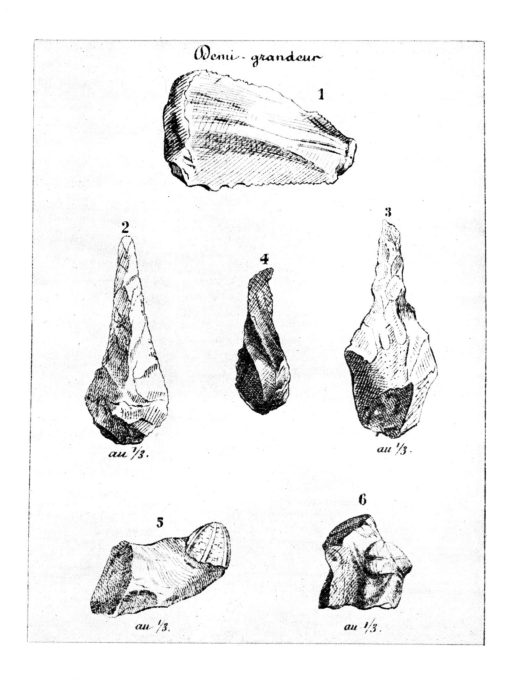

*Demi-grandeur*

1

2     4     3

*au ⅓.*     *au ⅓.*

5     6

*au ⅓.*     *au ⅓.*

*34. First contacts with prehistory. Paleolithic flints from Abbeville, reproduced in Jacques Boucher de Perthes,* Outils de pierre, *1865.*

*35. Opposite, the Victory of Samothrace, a large Hellenistic statue probably by Pythokritos of Rhodes, was discovered in 1863 and is now in the Louvre, Paris.*

archaeologists are assisted by specialists in various departments — architects, draftsmen, photographers, restorers, etc. Of course, not all the archaeological digs of the last hundred years, or even in some cases those being carried on at present, have been or are so ideally equipped as a collective undertaking utterly efficient on the technical plane. But major operations which have occupied some years, or those still in progress (such as the exploration of Pergamon, Olympia, Delphi, the Acropolis and the Agora of Athens, Pompeii, and Herculaneum, not to mention the various important Oriental sites), could not have taken place, and would indeed be unimaginable, without a combination of ample funds, appropriate scientific institutions, sound organization, and a highly trained and numerous staff. Furthermore, the increasing use of scientific methods of identifying archaeological remains both above and below the surface of the ground and of controlling investigations characterizes the archaeology of today,

36. *View of the ancient Etruscan necropolis of Populonia. The drums of the tumulus tombs of San Cerbone were made of blocks of stone, and the small rooms had domed roofs. Excavated between 1908 and 1921.*

37. *Discoveries at Herculaneum. Excavation and restoration of a street and its buildings in 1933.*

involving strict programming and teamwork as well as the closest possible collaboration between archaeologists and technicians.

If we regard monumental remains and archaeological finds as historical documents, it follows that they must be treated with respect and their material conservation guaranteed. They must be considered as elements of the common patrimony of our civilization, just as much as manuscripts or incunabula, or any other precious rarity from the past. This represents a profound, not to say a total, change from the days when relics from ancient times, regardless of their influence on ideas or their value as models inspiring art and taste, were preserved or destroyed, collected or dispersed, in accordance with the unchecked personal whims of princes or private individuals. Little by little this change has affected the collective conscience of modern society, though, as we shall see, the reform is not yet complete and definitive. Hence State intervention to protect monuments and finds by means of laws and organizations directed to that end; hence also the carrying-out of systematic restoration, and the development of the big public museums, open to all for study and enjoyment.

The highest interests of archaeology, at least where the whole of the nineteenth century is concerned, still seemed to be mainly identified with the knowledge of classical art and civilization. The excavations carried out in the main centers of Greek and Roman tradition contributed to a general revival of the study of classical antiquity, not only in the artistic field, but also in that of epigraphy,

38, 39. Archaeological exploration outside Europe. Above, view of the Roman city of Timgad in Algeria. Right,
triangular gate of the Mayan palace at
Palenque, Mexico.

political and economic history, topography, and the growth of cities. Tremendous works of exploration and restoration were undertaken — in Athens, Rome, the Campagna. Famous cities and sanctuaries were uncovered in Asia, many of them previously little more than names (such as Ephesus, Miletus, Pergamon, Priene, Baalbek); in Greece itself (Eleusis, Delphi, Olympia, Delos, Dodona, etc.); in Italy, North Africa, and Roman Europe. Pieces of sculpture were found which constituted landmarks in the history of Greek art, from the archaic sculpture of Ionia, Athens, and Delphi to the Praxiteles Hermes of Olympia, the Victory of Samothrace, and the magnificent reliefs of the Mausoleum of Halicarnassus and the Altar of Pergamon. The labor was shared enthusiastically by archaeologists of the major European countries, and soon by Americans as well. It is still in full spate, and shows no sign of coming to an early end.

Meanwhile, however, as archaeology established positive and autonomous methods of historical inquiry applicable to any past civilizations of even greater remoteness, it tended to break its original links with the Graeco-Roman world, and to widen its range more and more, both in space and in time. We have already seen that from the beginning of the nineteenth century European researchers were attracted to the great buried civilizations of the Near East, the cradle of history. As we draw nearer to our own day, we find archaeologists turning their attention with increasing zeal to the countries of the East — and the whole of ancient Egypt's past history, covering thousands of years, is laid bare. One need only mention the important work done round the pyramids of Giza and Saqqara, at Tell-el-Amarna, and in the temples and tombs of Thebes. The same is true of the Sumerian civilization (at Ur, Larsa, and Uruk), of Babylonia, Assyria, Syria, Anatolia (at Alaca Hüyük, the Hittite capital Boghaz-köy, and Troy), Elam, and Persia. We have mentioned the light thrown by Schliemann on Greek protohistory; the discovery of the Minoan civilization of Crete at the beginning of the present century completed its resurrection. Nor is that all; by the middle of the nineteenth century archaeologists and naturalists were already peering into the bottomless abysses of time, initiating the collection and study of the traces left by primitive humanity long before the existence of traditions or written records, not merely thousands but tens and hundreds of thousands of years ago, as far back as the very beginning of the stone age. Thus prehistory was born. And, finally, modern man's insatiable curiosity has led him beyond the confines of the Old World into the continents outside Europe — Central Asia and the Far East, Africa, the islands of Oceania, and Pre-Columbian America. The still incomplete exploration of distant lands and peoples, whose culture is only imperfectly known even in its present state, has developed in conjunction with an interest in the buried remains of their earlier cultural phases. Archaeology can be said to have followed in the wake of ethnology, in a continuous intermingling of the co-ordinates of space and time.

# ARCHAEOLOGY FOR "NON=PROFESSIONAL" MOTIVES:

## *FOR LOVE OF THE SUBJECT, FOR MATERIAL GAIN,*

## *FOR CULTURAL REASONS*

## The improved status of archaeology

Half a century ago, archaeology was still an obscure concept, expressed by an awkward word. Lying outside the interests of the more advanced literary and sociological culture, practically ignored by the learned world and the press, it never entered the thoughts of the average man, nor even those of the intellectual except for a very narrow circle of specialists. The archaeologist was one of those eccentric and somewhat pathetic types who provided material for caricature in the pages of Anatole France or the drawings of humorous periodicals. But this viewpoint was based on reality; one calls to mind, for example, the solitary figure of Paolo Orsi (one of the most distinguished men of that period) walking for mile after mile among the harsh rocks and beneath the burning sun of Sicily, in his impeccable dark suit and complete with umbrella, in search of a ruin or a tomb. Strange creatures they were; venerable bearded personages pursuing remote and useless curiosities. Who does not remember, in the still recent past, the familiar exclamation of new acquaintances, surprised to encounter a young and lively scholar: "What — *you* an archaeologist?"

Nowadays things have changed, or have turned completely round. Particularly since World War II, archaeology has taken giant strides in the knowledge and awareness not only of men of culture but also of the general public, and of the masses who derive both pleasure and food for thought from newspapers, periodicals, best-sellers, the radio, and television. Excavations and sensational finds now make headlines almost as big as sporting events, crime reports, and the private lives of actors and actresses. Their retrospective fascination has been described in the phrase "the romance of archaeology"; their problems are familiar to all, even to those who have never pursued classical studies. But there is better — or, perhaps, worse — in store. Rummaging about in the earth and picking up antiquities is no longer regarded as the pleasure or privilege of a few devotees and experts, but as the avowed hobby or the secret passion of all kinds of people, belonging to every profession and every social class. Troops of voluntary workers, constantly increasing in number, collaborate with or rival the competent authorities in archaeological exploration and the recovery of antiquities. The pharmacist who digs for prehistoric flint tools in France, the amateur frogmen who fish up Roman amphoras along the Tyrrhenian beaches, the peasant who unearths Etruscan tombs on his small farm, the clerk who buys pottery or statuettes, the diplomat who fills the diplomatic bag with archaeological souvenirs of the country which gives him hospitality — all have an ardent, almost a feverish passion for collecting antiquities. Each in his own way finds himself to be an archaeologist by avocation, and feels that he is in some small measure a follower of Schliemann. Collecting is practiced more widely; the trade in antiquities seems to prosper as never before.

Naturally, this vogue is of interest to governments, institutions, and competent persons, who can derive satisfaction from it insofar as it indicates a rise in the cultural level and an increase in its extent. Universal efforts are therefore made to encourage the development of the fashion, by means of more clearly arranged exhibits in archaeological museums, a more attractive layout of ruins and sites, the preparation of exhibitions, publicity handouts, and so on. Moreover, we should not forget that the tourist trade's energetic pursuit of archaeological attractions — in addition to the traditional ones of works of art and natural scenery — has meant a great deal to the economy of individual countries. But all this has its negative side, its element of danger, as far as the primary ends of archaeology are concerned. These, as we know, are now identical with those of historical science, and are only partly represented by the common man's conception of archaeological interests and activities, or by those aspects of archaeology which win public recognition. Indeed, these may even run counter to its true aims. Much confusion and misunderstanding may be said to exist with regard to the dividing line between science and culture, between disinterested appreciation and speculation.

It may be useful, therefore, to clarify the different aspects presented by the world of archaeology today, distinguishing as sharply as possible between its scientific and its nonscientific interests. The present chapter is devoted to examining the latter, which we might also call its "profane" or "non-professional" side — an aspect ignored in most of the books and articles on archaeology published during recent years. Because of the fact that such "lay" interests exist and flourish, and are, indeed, legitimate in their own sphere, they should not be disregarded. Nevertheless, they belong in the main to an instinctive propensity, to a different mentality and a different kind of purpose, usually subordinate and inferior to those of archaeology as a science, that is, as the winning of knowledge. The search for

COLORPLATE III. *Burial chamber in the Tomb of Tutankhamon in the Valley of the Kings. The tomb of the young pharaoh with its magnificent treasures was discovered by Howard Carter and Lord Carnarvon in 1922. Egyptian Museum, Cairo.*

antiquities as salable merchandise, or as sources of individual pleasure (or even of cultural or ideological inspiration), constituted an essential spur to the activities of archaeologists in past times. Today it remains — or should remain — marginal to research directed purely to scholarly ends; and if recent tendencies toward a "popularized" archaeology have revived any manifestations of it, whether disinterested or otherwise, it seems all the more essential to examine individual actions and motives, to point out their limitations and even, where necessary, to condemn frankly their machinations.

### Treasure hunting

In 1881, an extraordinary discovery was made in the necropolis of Thebes in Egypt. A burial chamber was opened in which were found, heaped up helter-skelter together with many other objects, the mummies of some of the most famous of the Egyptian pharaohs of the New Kingdom, together with their queens, princes, and high officials. These were taken to Cairo, and inspired Pierre Loti to write some of his most evocative pages (*La Mort de Philae*), worthy of a place in an anthology of "spine-chilling" literature. Nowadays they can be seen by purchasing a special ticket (costing somewhat more than admission to the whole museum); thus any tourist can, if he wishes, be admitted to the presence of people who in their own day, some three thousand years ago, lived isolated in the mystery of a sacredness that transcended the human, and for whom were prepared sumptuous and inaccessible tombs; figures of unlimited power who have entered into history and legend, such as Ahmose, the liberator of Egypt and founder of the Eighteenth Dynasty, Tuthmosis III, the conqueror of Asia, and Ramesses II, whose name and effigy are carved on all the monuments of the Nile Valley from the Delta to Nubia. Here, through an accident absolutely unique in the history of mankind, we possess not simply records or works but the makers of history themselves in their almost intact physical reality, gathered together as if for an apocalyptic rendezvous. And this is due, in the last analysis, to an almost commonplace event connected with the activity of very early "treasure seekers."

In a country where the dead were, with meticulous care, surrounded with every luxury and comfort for their consolation beyond the grave, the sacrilegious pillaging of tombs was often a kind of exasperated vengeance for the poverty of the living — as it were, a primitive form of economic-social vindication. Particularly during the period of Egyptian decadence, tomb robbers became more and more numerous. They organized themselves into bands and formed raiding parties against which not only the forces of authority but even religious awe gradually became powerless. Striking evidence has survived of this "treasure hunting" in tombs — for example, the records of a trial held in Thebes in the time of Ramesses IX, about 1100 B.C., of a

40. *Emil Brugsch and Gaston Maspero at the entrance to the secret cache at Deir el Bahari (from* The Century, *New York, May 1887). Here they found the mummies of some of the greatest pharaohs of ancient Egypt, concealed by the priests to protect them from tomb robbers.*

gang who had plundered the pyramid of the ancient pharaoh Sebek-emsaf II and a number of tombs belonging to private individuals. Here is a passage from the deposition of the accused, concerning the robbery of the royal tomb (J. H. Breasted, *Ancient Records of Egypt*, IV, pp. 265 ff.):

We opened their coffins and their coverings in which they were. We found this august mummy of this king.... There was a numerous list of amulets and ornaments of gold at its throat; its head had a mask of gold upon it; the august mummy of this king was overlaid with gold throughout. Its coverings were wrought with gold and silver, within and without; inlaid with every splendid costly stone. We stripped off the gold, which we found on the august mummy of this god, and its amulets and ornaments which were at its throat, and the coverings wherein it rested. [We] found the King's-Wife likewise; we stripped off all that we found on her likewise. We set fire to their coverings. We stole their furniture, which we found with them, being vases of gold, silver and bronze. We divided, and made the gold which we found on these two gods, on their mummies, and the amulets, ornaments and coverings, into eight parts.

Since the monumental tombs and even the great underground

41. *The Treasure Seeker. Seventeenth-century painting of the Dutch School in the Museum of Fine Arts, Budapest.*

chambers were no longer safe, in spite of every kind of concealment and subterfuge, the authorities tried at least to preserve the bodies of the kings themselves from destruction. We know that the mummy of Ramesses II was moved a number of times, under the threat of constantly increasing dangers. In the end, during the Twenty-second Dynasty, it was decided to collect together his remains and those of other great pharaohs in a modest and provisional resting place which managed to escape detection and succeeded in preserving them till our own day. Without such precautions, they would have been lost thousands of years ago.

Not only Egypt, but the whole of the ancient world experienced the activities of tomb robbers (in Greek, *tymborychoi*). Modern archaeologists constantly encounter the results of their work in the course of excavations. It is very seldom that graves of any importance are found absolutely intact, or show no signs of having been tampered with (apart from reconstruction work), or at least of attempted burglary. Even where the funerary furnishings — vases, fragments of furniture, weapons, etc. — are preserved, they have usually been disarranged and rummaged through, and the objects of greatest value are missing: the jewels of the deceased, which were always the main objective of the robbers because of their intrinsic value and immediate salability. In this respect, the despoiling of tombs is no different from the sacking of cities and temples, a frequent occurrence in the event of war or invasion. For example, the same barbarian tribes from Gaul who had plundered the sanctuary of Delphi in 279 B.C. turned their attention, a few years later, when they were in the pay of Pyrrhus, to excavating with impunity the royal tombs of Aegae in Macedonia, and carried off all their treasures (Diodorus Siculus, XXII, 12). All the same, even in antiquity there were already indications of a certain awareness of the archaeological and artistic value of the objects discovered in tombs, with the result that the *tymborychoi* themselves began to direct their activities toward exploiting this new interest and source of profit. (We have already seen this in connection with the excavations in the necropolis of Corinth in the time of Caesar.)

Quite apart from tombs, there are countless other cases of hidden wealth, consecrated to divinities, or buried by private individuals to preserve it from sudden danger and later abandoned and lost. In such cases, its recovery takes on the character of a trick of fortune; it has an aura of mystery, stirring the popular imagination and assuming a legendary quality. With all peoples and in all periods, the idea of treasure is instinctively linked with that of "fortune," but it also implies the idea of the "past," in the sense of a past not recorded in history but "discovered." To find or to seek treasure is already, if you like, archaeology in embryo — a rudimentary and popular archaeology making no distinction between the jewels in an ancient tomb and the buried gold of pirates, knowing of no other interests or rights outside those of the finder; and yet containing within itself that longing for the unforeseen, that passion for investigation and desire for discovery, which represent the basic motivation of true archaeological activity. In this context, the writer cannot forget the deep emotion of all those — from the humble finders to the authorities and the scholars — who had occasion to see and handle the heap of gold coins, ancient and modern, which poured from a hole in a wall during the demolition of a house in the Via Alessandrina in Rome in 1931, when the Via dell'Impero was being opened up. Yet this treasure, which gave rise to complicated judiciary proceedings, had only been hidden since the end of the last century.

Conversely, archaeology has never been able to detach itself entirely from the appeal of the picturesque world of tomb violators and treasure seekers. For a very long time, as we already know, a love of antiquities and the desire to rediscover the past were conceived exclusively, or nearly so, in terms of the recovery and collection of objects dug out of the ground. Official scholarship concentrated its attention on individual "pieces," considered from the point of view of their illustrative, mythological, or artistic significance, independent of the context in which they were found. The best objects were picked out, and all the rest disregarded or destroyed. The first excavators of Herculaneum penetrated to the level

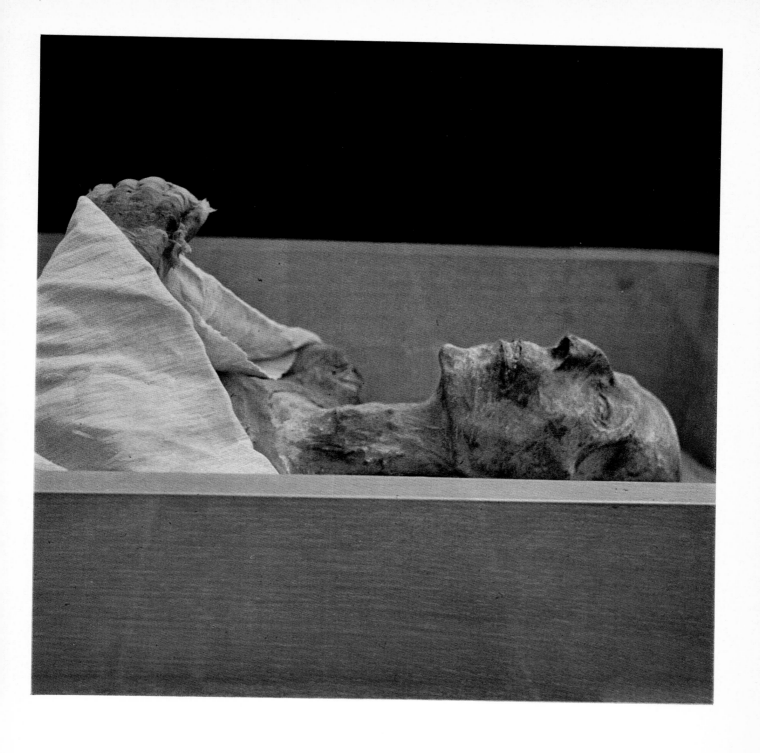

COLORPLATE IV. *Head of the mummy of Ramesses II discovered in the cache of royal mummies at Deir el Bahari and preserved in the Egyptian Museum, Cairo.*

of the ancient city, buried under the debris of Vesuvius, through a network of tunnels piercing the walls of the buildings, which enabled them to remove vast quantities of sculpture, bronzes, and furnishings of every kind, destined to become the pride of the Bourbon Museum. In the first half of the nineteenth century, the burial grounds of Vulci and Cerveteri were pillaged wholesale in the hope of finding painted vases and articles made of gold, without any concern for the tombs themselves and for the integrity of their furnishings.

But even apart from these extreme cases, well known in the history of archaeological research, the general attitude until the more recent establishment of modern scientific concepts (and often today still outside scholarly circles) has been to regard excavation as an enterprise exploiting the subsoil in order to extract from it material for collections and museums; material sought for its rarity, curiosity, and artistic merit, but also for its market value (which came to the same thing in the end). The demands of the dealer in antiquities have provided — and still do — an irresistible incentive for uncontrolled search and depredations in nearly all countries rich in archaelogical remains, encouraging the activities of clandestine excavators, casual or professional, who operate exclusively for gain and are the true descendants of the ancient *tymborychoi*. On the other hand, it is not unusual to find that even public authorities seem to be inspired by the notion of protecting and regulating the "ownership" of antique objects considered essentially from the point of view of their value as an inheritance, or that they still equate archaeological discoveries with the finding of "treasure."

Of course, modern investigations of a more responsible nature, aiming above all at the acquisition of historical data, definitely allot second place to the recovery of "museum pieces" when conducting excavations, and in any case reject the isolation and selection of the most significant objects from the rest of the material unearthed.

All the same, it is clear that even today, deep in his heart, every archaeologist, however self-controlled and austere, harbors a dream — to alight one day through a stroke of fortune on the outstanding discovery, the precious object, the unique document, the incomparable work of art which will forever bear his own name: in fact, in the last analysis, he too dreams of "treasure."


## Collecting

The history of archaeology is closely interwoven with that of the collecting of antiquities. The divers activities and aspects of the collecting habit reflect, sometimes in an odd way, the various modern attitudes toward antique objects.

At the bottom of every kind of collecting there lies, as everyone knows, a kind of imponderable urge, a divine fire, which without

42, 43. *Renaissance collection of antiquities. Above, the courtyard of the Palazzo Valle-Capranica in Rome. Engraving by H. Cock, 1553. Below, the garden-museum of Jacopo Galli in Rome. Drawing from a sketchbook of M. van Heemskerck, 1532-36.*

any logical reason seems to drive certain dedicated men irresistibly on to seek and acquire particular objects. This mania is perhaps as old as civilization itself; we are acquainted with unmistakable signs of it since Roman times. The works of Cicero, Pliny, and others describe in lively terms a society permeated by the craze for collecting Greek works of art and old curios. Cicero himself shows an exaggerated impatience to obtain possession of "pieces" commissioned from his friend Atticus ("I await them with longing," "give the matter your whole attention," "send them with the utmost speed," "the mere thought of them gives me delight," "My heartfelt thanks" in his letters *Ad Atticum*, I, 9, 2; 11, 3; 3, 2, etc.). Then, as now, auction sales flourished, antique dealers fixed high prices, fakes were circulated among the less shrewd collectors, the vanity of the newly rich was exploited. Sometimes even stratagems and tricks were resorted to in order to obtain possession of an object, as in the case

44. *Un Cabinet d'Amateur de Tableaux, painting by Frans Francken the Younger (1581-1642). Musée des Beaux-Arts, Antwerp.*

45. *The Loggia dei Lanzi, Piazza Signoria, Florence, with classical, Renaissance, and nineteenth-century sculpture side by side. Sculpture has stood in the Loggia since the sixteenth century.*

of Verres, the notorious despoiler of Sicily. Even when he visited one of his own defense lawyers, the latter had to set the servants to guard his silver (Cicero, *In Verrem*, II, IV, 13, 33).

The covetousness of collectors can assume abnormal proportions when they have unlimited wealth and power. Thus, for example, were established the vast private museum of Asinius Pollio in antiquity, that of the Farnese family during the Renaissance, and that of the Torlonia family during the nineteenth century. As an example of uncontrolled and indiscriminate collecting mania, one can quote the Italian tenor Egon Gorga, who reduced himself to bankruptcy in the first ten years of the present century by accumulating every kind of object — mainly archaeological material, but also folk art, furniture of various periods, musical instruments, and surgical and scientific instruments (now the property of the State). It was an ill-assorted collection, in which sheer quantity — the mere fact of

46. *The original establishment of the National Museum in Naples, the largest collection of classical antiquities in the world. The scene pictures the solemn transfer of the Bourbon collections from the royal villa of Portici to the Neapolitan palace in 1822. From a contemporary engraving.*

having amassed just as much as possible — far outweighed quality.

In collecting, "possession" is an absolute and determining objective which can override any other consideration, moral or cultural. Like the Romans after the conquest of Greece, conquerors in the modern world have often compelled the vanquished to hand over works of art, and collections of art and archaeology, beginning with the famous tribute of antique masterpieces exacted from Pius VI by Napoleon with the Treaty of Tolentino in 1797. Similar events occurred during World War II: for example, the transferring from Berlin to Russia of the Hellenistic sculptures from the Altar of Pergamon (since voluntarily returned). Every country tries to enrich its own museums by every possible means. It even happens that within the same country, even the same city, individual museums contend fiercely for the possession of certain objects, without any logical reason. Directors of public collections sometimes show the same acquisitive desires and the same ridiculous jealousies as private collectors.

Clearly, such a universal passion cannot be explained simply in terms of pure material interests. The possessive instinct, the desire, even if subconscious, to own a treasure, undoubtedly acts as a powerful stimulus. There is also the deliberate intention of hoarding or making an investment (though this applies rather to the collecting of pictures, coins, and jewelry than to archaeological finds). The smaller collectors in particular more or less consistently cherish hopes of gain. Furthermore, because of the demand, there has grown up around collecting a complicated network of economic values, commercial links, and speculative activities which foster the antiquarian

*47, 48. Early nineteenth-century collections of antiquities. Left, a room in the Villa Borghese in Rome. Right, the dome of Sir John Soane's Museum, London.*

market at a local, national, and international level. But as a rule it is not primarily the desire for gain that impels people to collect antique objects, but rather a disinterested delight in them, sometimes colored by a touch of idealism, by personal or collective taste, a love of culture, curiosity, vanity, or caprice.

Based on this diffuse and fluctuating psychological propensity, more definite motives develop of an intellectual or social nature according to the period, the setting, or the circumstances. Thus, during the Renaissance (as again later during the Neoclassical period), antique statues were collected in homage to a certain ideal of beauty to be rediscovered or imitated. In the seventeenth and eighteenth centuries, however, a pedantic and erudite curiosity prevailed, leading to the formation of those "cabinets of antiquities" in which marble sculpture, bronzes, and antique vases mingled with natural history collections and bizarre objects (a typical example is the Museo Kircheriano, founded, as already noted, by Kircher at the Collegio Romano). The modern archaeological museum, which on the one hand arises out of the specific needs of scientific documentation, tends on the other toward specialization and the dividing of the collections according to material, period, or cultural region. Many of the great collections of the past grew out of the cult of civic memories, the pride of illustrious families or individuals, or a desire for prestige on the part of a particular ruler or nation.

Between the sixteenth and the nineteenth centuries, an essentially aristocratic conception of antiquarian collecting prevailed. Throughout Europe, magnificent princely collections were formed, or others established by wealthy private citizens (these included such famous names as Farnese, Ludovisi, Barberini, Borghese, Albani, Arundel, Soane, Campana, De Luynes, Blacas, Pourtalès, Rothschild, Stroganoff, Fol). Practically speaking, the public museums themselves depended mainly during this period on the munificence of sovereigns and popes, and did not differ substantially in character from the princely collections. Minor private collectors were almost without exception travelers or excavators who supplied the great collectors.

But as archaeology grew increasingly scientific and came under the legislative protection of the State, as the noble families declined and the great private fortunes diminished, as the structure of society grew more national and democratic, the public museum has gradually become established during the last century, and particularly our own, as a model and guide for the collecting and conservation of antiquities. Much of the property of the great private collections has finally found its way into the major State or city museums, or has been made available to the public in some way. Some of these collections have acquired a size and character which have earned them a world-wide reputation (for example, the Vatican Museum, the National Museum at Naples, the Louvre, the National Archaeological Museum in Madrid, the British Museum, the Hermitage, the National Museum in Athens, the Cairo Museum, the Metropolitan Museum, New York).

At the same time, the field of private collecting has gradually narrowed and tended to disintegrate. It survives only at the highest level, in a few anachronistic remains of old collections (including the Torlonia collections in Rome, and those of some of the great English country houses), or as part of the cultural interests of certain financiers and industrialists. It has come within reach of the middle classes in more unassuming forms, according to the tastes and particular interests of individual collectors, their hope of making a good investment, or their desire for status symbols.

Today, therefore, the cultural and worldly motives which combined to create the great humanistically inspired collections of the past seem to be directed into two often opposing channels — the public museum, scientific in character, and the small private collection of a dilettante nature.


### Delusions, deceptions, counterfeits

A very interesting chapter in the history of collecting can be written on the subject of forgeries. A whole literature exists on the theme, especially on the counterfeiting of works of art; exceedingly instructive exhibitions devoted to the latter have been held recently. Even the phenomenon of forgeries leads us back to antiquity. Inexpert collectors, the newly rich of Imperial Rome with a taste for ostentation, were often tricked by wily dealers into buying pictures, sculp-

49. A typical eighteenth-century imitation of classical painting. This fresco depicting Jupiter and Ganymede, by A. R. Mengs, was transferred onto canvas. National Gallery of Antiquities, Rome.

ture, or silverware which were copies or of no value, in the belief that they were works by famous Greek artists — and were made to pay for them accordingly. The caustic Martial, who knew all about forgers, wrote the following lines to one of them, who boasted of possessing a genuine piece of engraved silver from Mys: "The more genuine it is, the less it has anything to do with you!" (*Epigrams*, VIII, 34). It was particularly easy to pass off "antique" objects supposed to have some connection with famous persons or heroes. Such things were in great demand by the public, who could be deluded that they were drinking from the cup of Nestor, or possessed the bronze bowl in which Sisyphus had washed his feet (Horace, *Satires*, II, 3). Delusions of this kind, more or less ingenuous, are found at all periods, varying according to the prevailing mentality and culture — from the countless false relics of the Middle Ages, spontaneously accepted by popular piety, to the gigantic archaeological and artistic frauds of the modern world.

In truth, the phenomenon of forgery (which is basically a matter

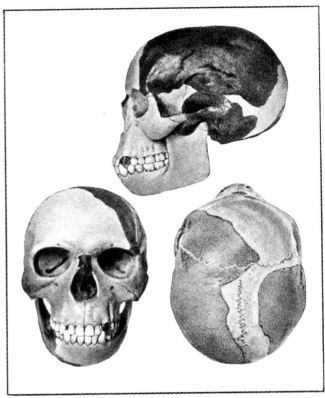

*50, 51. Famous forgeries of modern archaeology. Left, the so-called Tiara of Saitaphernes, an imitation of Graeco-Scythian goldwork of the third century B.C., acquired by the Louvre in 1896. Right, the "prehistoric" skull from Piltdown, artfully reconstructed from heterogeneous elements.*

of deceptive attribution) cannot be reduced simply to deliberate mystification for the sake of dishonest material gain, as in the obvious case of modern forgeries of works by great painters — Vermeer, Corot, Van Gogh — widely diffused throughout art markets and acquired not only by private collectors but even by museums. This profit motive applies mainly to the faking of works of art because of the immediate sale value, usually at a known price, of certain classes of such things, and of certain well-attested artists' signatures. The situation is similar in the case of valuables, when an imitation is substituted for the authentic object.

We encounter in addition, however, a whole range of reasons, motives, attitudes, sentiments, of considerable variety and many shades, which favor errors and deceptions, contributing to an increase in the counterfeiting of documents, finds, and relics of the past. In the first place, it is well known how much importance was accorded during the Renaissance to copies and imitations of antique sculpture, as well as its restoration and completion. These were executed for love of the great models which inspired contemporary taste, without any intent to deceive. Some of these imitations, particularly small bronze groups and statuettes like those by Pier Jacopo Bonacolsi (known as "l'Antico"), could be mistaken in their own day or later for classical originals; and a love of hoaxing, characteristic of artistic circles, even induced Michelangelo to bury a marble Cupid of his own making and dig it up again later as an "antique" (Vasari, *Lives*, de Vere edition, vol. IX, p. 12).

Nowadays we clearly distinguish between the reproduction of a work of art made for scientific, didactic, or decorative purposes, as

80

COLORPLATE V. *The Muse Polyhymnia, encaustic painting on slate. Probably an eighteenth-century imitation of the antique. Museum of the Etruscan Academy, Cortona.*

52-54. *Modern forgeries of Etruscan terra cottas. Left, one of the huge warriors in the Metropolitan Museum of Art, New York. Center, the Kore of the Ny Carlsberg Glyptothek, Copenhagen. Right, the Diana in the St. Louis City Art Museum, probably by Alceo Dossena.*

a "souvenir," and the deceptive and fraudulent fake. But there was a time when this distinction was not nearly so clear, when artists and even archaeologists, totally immersed in the objects of their admiration and study, did not hesitate to add to or complete, even to "re-make," antique articles. This explains the phenomenon, so general and widespread during the sixteenth and seventeenth centuries, of scholars creating apocryphal documents, artificial texts, sham antique inscriptions, and false coins. It is impossible to say whether they were more strongly motivated by an inordinate enthusiasm for their own erudition, the enjoyment of a pedantic joke, or a vainglorious pleasure in displaying their skill; the idea of material gain was certainly the last to occur to them.

All things considered, some of the great archaeological practical jokes of more recent times are latter-day ploys in the same vein, particularly in the tricky field of prehistory. Objects of stone and bone were already being produced in the last century, sometimes with counterfeit engraved decoration, such as those fraudulently deposited in the caves of Chaffaud in France, or a cavern near Thayngen in Switzerland. It is understandable that the impact on both the general public and the world of learning by the discovery of man-made objects going back to the earliest Quaternary period, along with the remains of extinct animals, could create an atmosphere of disorientation and uncertainty in which anything, however strange, becomes plausible and deception thrives. The revelation of paleolithic art, of such astonishing realism, led in some ways to the same consequences as the discovery of classical art during the Renaissance, namely, the desire to attempt imitations of it, and to circulate such imitations. It is also interesting to study the opposite side of the coin: the incredulity of scholars when faced with apparently improbable discoveries, such as the painted cave of Altamira in Spain in 1879. (It was more than twenty years before the good faith of its discoverer, Marcelino de Sautuola, was recognized.) A similar instance has occurred recently in connection with the paleolithic paintings and engravings in the cave of Rouffignac in the Dordogne — which, incidentally, has been known for centuries. The suspicion of faking gave rise to a violent scientific and journalistic polemic which had the whole of France in an uproar in 1956, and which ended in a verdict of authenticity, unanimously sanctioned by the greatest international authorities in the field of prehistoric art.

The well-known fossil of the skull of a primitive man discovered in pieces at Piltdown, Sussex, in 1911 and 1912, and regarded by scholars for forty years as a landmark in the reconstruction of the races of mankind in the Quaternary period, was declared in 1953 in the Bulletin of the British Museum to be a fake. It was in fact a prehistoric human brain-pan combined with the jaw of a chimpanzee. Another notorious instance of archaeological forgery in our own century is that of Glozel, near Vichy, where in 1924 shells and tiles with traces of writing, attributed to the neolithic period, began to come to light. From this an attempt was made to deduce no less than the Western origin, at a very remote period, of the alphabet. The discussion which arose out of this discovery was all the more serious in that it involved a group of very eminent French archaeologists, members of the Institut, who supported the claims of these outlandish falsifications.

The originator of the Glozel deception was simply an ignorant but very crafty countryman in pursuit of the meager profit to be derived from charging an entrance fee to see his "finds," and supported by an ambitious and unscrupulous doctor who procured the models for him. This is a typical example of "popular" and clumsy counterfeiting by peasant forgers, which does not by any means deceive only the unlearned, as is demonstrated also by the thorny problem of the "Centuripe workshop" still operating in Sicily and producing a vast output of painted terra cottas of the oddest shapes and designs, some of which manage to take in even distinguished scholars.

Naturally, the problem of forgeries becomes a more urgent one when it passes into the realm of "learned" counterfeits, the products of technical and stylistic knowledge of a high order, among which can be included many of the artistic fakes passed off successfully during the past ten years. In the more successful cases (for the forger), the verdict is disputed — the sculptured marble "throne" of Boston, for example, supposedly a Greek work of the fifth century B.C. — or the deception may even remain completely undetected. As far as the art of antiquity is concerned, we could include in this category some eighteenth-century paintings, like the famous

Muse of Cortona and other works attributed with certainty to good artists of the period, such as Giuseppe Guerra and Anton Raphael Mengs. At the end of the last century, the Louvre bought the splendid "Tiara of Saitaphernes," apparently Graeco-Scythian work of gold with decoration in relief; it later turned out to be by an extremely skillful Russian goldsmith. Our own century has witnessed the brilliant work of Alceo Dossena in imitating modern and antique works, poised on the borderline between speculation and a passion for art. He possessed the talent of an eclectic designer and was endowed with an unsurpassed capacity for absorbing the "style" of any artist or period whatsoever.

Generally, the focusing of official scientific attention on some particular artistic or archaeological problem sparks off an immediate reaction on the part of the forgers. We have already seen this in the case of prehistory (and the same phenomenon had manifested itself even earlier with Renaissance classicism and with Neoclassicism). The "Tiara of Saitaphernes" was certainly a consequence of the magnificent finds discovered in the ancient cities of the Crimea. Interest in the Etruscan world and Etruscan art has in recent decades resulted in a greater concentration of forgeries in this area. Between 1916 and 1920, pieces of enormous terra-cotta figures of warriors were shipped to the United States from an Orvieto workshop and for thirty-odd years figured among the masterpieces of the Metropolitan Museum of New York. A recent official statement has clearly and definitely relegated them to a place among modern impostures. The same verdict awaits other "Etruscan" terra cottas in various museums throughout the world (the subject of fierce polemics, and already practically condemned by the openly expressed opinions of scholars), such as the "Maiden" of Copenhagen or the St. Louis Diana, artifacts in the manner of the Apollo of Veii and other similar antique works.

Archaeological forgeries have become particularly plentiful and widespread in our own day, in proportion to the increasing popularization of archaeological excavations and the passion for collecting. The tricks of the manufacturers of antiquities, bronzes, terra cottas, vases, ivories, goldsmiths' work (even at a fairly low technical and cultural level), and of their wily distributors, are aimed in particular at those who collect on a moderate or small scale. But it should be pointed out that they find a ready reception because of the singular psychology of the purchasers, who often, because of their dilettante approach, tend to let the pleasure of buying outweigh prudence and judgment — ignoring expert advice, or only seeking it when the purchase has already been made, and even then secretly continuing to cherish their own illusion. Once again, then, we find the same irrational element flourishing — the same illusion which encouraged counterfeiting in earlier times, and which, when all is said and done, gives this phenomenon its own unmistakable significance among the contradictory aspects of our modern culture.

## Speculation and the safeguarding of the archaeological patrimony

In the center of ancient Rome, in the valley of the Forum and on the site of the Comitia, there existed a small area, mysterious and venerated, and already by the end of the Republican era paved with black stone, a funereal color, according to Roman authors, signifying the site of the tomb of Romulus, the founder of the city. The excavations carried out between 1899 and 1900 by Giacomo Boni beneath the Lapis Niger brought to light a whole series of stone foundations, architectural remains, a deposit of pottery and votive statuettes going back to the sixth century B.C., and a cippus with an archaic Latin inscription, all belonging without a doubt to a sacred area piously guarded throughout the vicissitudes of the centuries and finally sealed up by the reverence of posterity.

Archaeologists in particular, exploring ancient dwellings and sanctuaries, are constantly coming across evidence of the respect in which relics of a still more remote past were held. Even in the prehistoric caves we already find figures of animals traced beside or above other pre-existing figures, without crossing over them, or untouched sacrificial corners, which life, with its inexorable demands for destruction, had abandoned. Temples, tombs, and other monumental buildings of the ancient East and of the classical world were protected, restored, faithfully reconstructed in the same places and sometimes even in the same form. It is well known how much execration was heaped on the memory of Erostratus, the maniac who burned down the great temple of Artemis at Ephesus on the night that Alexander the Great was born. All this is obviously linked with conservatism or religious awe. But one also finds signs of human regard for the memory of ancestors, for civic glories, or for works of particular renown, beauty, or interest. Cicero remarks (*In Verrem*, II, IV, 57, 126) that the people of Syracuse were very sad at the sacking of their city, "firstly because of religious sentiment, and the firm belief that they should venerate and safeguard the paternal gods inherited from their forebears, and secondly because the Greeks are passionately devoted to beautiful things, to works of art, statues and paintings."

The earliest examples of public interest in the safeguarding of historic monuments and the passing of laws for their protection relate to Rome, particularly in the late period of the Empire. The Constantinian Constitution prohibited the removal of marble sculpture from urban buildings. Cassiodorus, as Theodoric's minister, created special offices for the conservation of monuments and the recovery of stolen works of art. Well on into the Middle Ages, the great remnants of ancient Rome such as Trajan's Column and the statue of Marcus Aurelius were still being protected and restored. The main threat to them was not so much the destroying fury of the barbarians (around which too many legends have been built up) as poverty and neglect, private and public depredations, and above all the increasing tendency to use the materials, ornaments, and furnishings for new constructions. Countermeasures, usually timid and ineffectual, were more concerned with the defense of a patrimony still regarded as "real" (i.e., of concrete objects) than with ideal and historical values.

Only in the Renaissance, as the passion for antique objects and the very concept of antiquity became clearly defined, was there the beginning of a system of archaeological tutelage in the modern sense. But the idea of protecting ancient monuments and ruins as such advanced slowly, in sharp contrast to the intensification of wholesale destruction involved in the building and town planning requirements that have already been mentioned. "But why should we grieve over the Goths, the Vandals, and the other perfidious enemies of the Latin name," writes Baldassare Castiglione, in a report sent by Raphael as commissioner of antiquities to Leo X, "if those very men who as fathers and guardians should defend these poor relics of Rome have themselves worked so long and strenuously to destroy and eradicate them? How many Pontiffs, Holy Father . . . have permitted the ruin and decay of the ancient temples, statues, arches, and other buildings, the glory of their founders? How much lime has been made out of antique statues and other ancient ornaments?" It was not until the centuries of the Enlightenment and the discipline of the art historian (the eighteenth and, still more, the nineteenth centuries) that this awareness became general and finally gained control. Even in recent times, however, and particularly in our own day, the destruction of ancient remains still goes on — because of public necessity or private speculation. (Even protective legislation, however severe, is often helpless against such things.)

Meanwhile, the intervention of the authorities was extended to include the prohibition or regulation of archaeological excavations: for example, in the Papal States, with the edicts of Cardinals Aldobrandini (1624), Sforza (1646), Altieri (1686), Spinola (1701), Albani (1733), Valenti (1750), Doria-Pamphili (1802, reproducing a decree of Pius VII), and finally the famous edict "On excavations and the conservation of monuments" of Cardinal Bartolomeo Pacca (1820) who, assembling and unifying all the complex data relating to protective measures, established the prototype of modern legislation in this field. In Tuscany there were the Grand Duke's rescripts of 1750, 1761, and 1780, which formulated the problems of the freedom of private individuals to carry out excavations, and of the ownership of finds, defining the rights of the State. In Austria, Napoleonic France, and the Kingdom of Italy similar measures were taken; in the Kingdom of the Two Sicilies, Ferdinand I issued decrees concerning ancient monuments and excavations (1822).

These preliminary moves, sometimes remarkably in advance of their time, came to maturity in the various European countries only in the second half of the nineteenth century or the beginning of the twentieth. A whole series of laws, varying in their provisions and sometimes in their spirit as well, was promulgated in defense of historical monuments and works of art, and for the regulation of

55. *A tomb opened by archaeological smugglers. The struggle of public organizations to defend the archaeological heritage from ruin and speculation is becoming increasingly fierce and difficult.*

archaeological discoveries and excavations, as well as for the setting up of administrative bodies for the exercise of this tutelage. The existing Italian laws (1902, 1909, 1939) and the Italian system of organization, which dates back to 1875, can be regarded as models of their kind, both for clarity of principles and efficacy of methods. They are based on the concept of public ownership of the archaeological subsoil and of finds, except for the rights of compensation of owners and finders. They also authorize State intervention through protective control over all historical, archaeological, and artistic buildings and objects which can in any way be considered, even when in private hands, to be of public concern. The work of protection in all its forms, and the carrying out or control of archaeological research, are entrusted to the Directorship-General of Antiquities and Fine Arts, which functions through the Soprintendenze alle Antichità (while responsibility for medieval and modern monuments and works of art rests with the Soprintendenze ai Monumenti e alle Gallerie). Similar organizations and juridical concepts are found in Greece (1932), Spain (1933–36), and Soviet Russia — that is, in the countries richest in antiquities — and they have spread, or are in process of spreading, to the countries of Eastern Europe, Africa,

*56. Protection of Trajan's Column in Rome during World War II. One of the pressing problems of modern states is the safeguarding of ancient monuments from war damage.*

and Asia. In France, the Germanic countries, and particularly in the Anglo-Saxon nations, the methods and regulations in force are based on a more modest degree of State intervention. The increasingly urgent need for an international system of control was finally laid down in the solemn "Recommendation" of UNESCO, adopted by the General Conference of New Delhi (1956).

The crucial point of the problem of protection is in fact the relationship between private and public rights. More and more during recent centuries, and in an increasingly decisive fashion today, the principle has been accepted, almost as an unquestionable requirement of our very civilization, that historical evidence and the products of man's genius in past ages should be respected and enjoyed as the patrimony not of individuals, but of us all. Archaeology in the learned age of humanism was still a private activity of scholarly and inquiring minds, of rich men and of princes. There still persists in many countries the widely held view that antique objects or works of art are possessions like any other, with exclusive right of ownership, so that the proprietor may, according to his whim, sell, conceal, or even destroy them, and that such goods can be freely "produced," taken from the ground, and made the subject of free speculation. Modern society, on the other hand, regarding them as objects of a very specialized nature, destined for universal admiration, study, and conservation for future generations, tends to impose limitations to a greater or lesser degree on private ownership, and on the exercise of private activities in their respect.

These opposing views give rise to a dramatic conflict, still unresolved, affecting attitudes of mind, customs, rights, and abuses — varying, of course, according to circumstances. On the one hand, for example, it seems almost incredible that in France some of the most famous paleolithic painted caves, unique monuments of the art of primitive man, should be owned by private individuals who are responsible for their care and maintenance and make a profit from admission charges; or that any amateur archaeologist should have the legal right to excavate, take possession of, and shut up in his own safe antique works of art — even when they are of exceptional worth — making it impossible for scholars to study them, and selling photographs of them at an exaggerated price. On the other hand, where legislation is stricter (as in Italy), one has to contend with ignorance of the laws, passive resistance to them, or illegal activity in the form of illicit excavations and an organized clandestine traffic in antiquities, with international ramifications and illegal export. This is fostered by a lack of understanding on the part of the public, the authorities, even of the magistracy, which is often hard to credit, and sets those responsible for safeguarding the nation's archaeological patrimony an extremely difficult task.

One particular aspect of the problem is the difficulty of preventing such works from being exported; in other words, of preserving the nation's artistic and archaeological inheritance. To prevent the dis-

COLORPLATE VI. *The Ruins of Agrigento. This engraving by Paul Sandby shows the site before the coming of archaeologists and tourists.*

persal of this wealth is a point of honor with every country, as well as being to its advantage. Regulations to this effect have existed since the eighteenth century. Today we see the new nations of Africa and Asia, which for some centuries have endured the archaeological depredations of Europeans, setting up rigorous barriers in the way of exportation. Claims are even being made in respect to relics which were alienated in the past, such as the famous series of antique sculptures from Greece now in British, French, and German museums. However, there is perhaps a tendency for these attitudes, both old and new, to be overcome as universalistic cultural horizons open wider. Eloquent symptoms of the change can be seen in the intensification of great archaeological exhibitions, traveling from country to country, and the increasing extent to which objects or specimens are exchanged between the archaeological institutes and museums of different nations. The treasures of the past are now beginning to be recognized as among the most worthy ambassadors of the individual traditions and culture of nations. Not only is the antique object no longer to be considered a source of private and personal enjoyment alone; it is not even the exclusive patrimony of a single national community, but is tending to become established as the property of all mankind.

In these tendencies is rooted the need to set things of historical and artistic value outside and above the conflict of national self-interest. During the two world wars, in particular, the most civilized nations vied with one another in providing for the material protection of their own monuments and museums with all the technical devices at their command. Yet this did not succeed in preventing irreparable losses through bombing, fire, and depredations. To quote examples in Italy alone, one can mention the Roman ships at Nemi, the museum of Marzabotto in Emilia, and a considerable part of the collections of the Capua and Ancona museums. It has thus become clear that the problem must be tackled at an international level, and that there must be a moral undertaking in respect to the works of the past, in all circumstances, given in the same spirit of instinctive humanity and supreme neutrality which accepts and controls, in a different field, the activities of the Red Cross. Such an undertaking would be implemented by the United Nations, aided by new legislation, but mainly guaranteed, of course, by the civic consciences of individual nations. There is, for example, the successful effort, promoted by UNESCO, to save the Egyptian rock temples of Abu Simbel from the consequences of constructing the Aswan Dam.


## The tourist trade

A number of the subjects already discussed — collecting, counterfeiting, the antiquarian trade, the safeguarding of monuments, etc.

57. W. Tischbein's Portrait of Goethe
(detail). Staedelsches Kunstinstitut,
Frankfort.

— are as closely concerned with the world of medieval and modern
art as with that of archaeology (a distinction, by the way, which
has a meaning within the orbit of our European civilization, but
appears less clear-cut where the history of the other continents is
concerned). This is particularly true of the problems connected with
the tourist industry. The attraction that countries rich in historic
monuments and works of art exert on foreigners depends mainly,
in its traditional and, so to speak, "nineteenth-century" aspect, on the
works of the great masters. There is no doubt that the Louvre is
visited far more often for the sake of the Mona Lisa than for the
Stele of Hammurabi or the Winged Victory of Samothrace. In the
eyes of the world, Venice is a more celebrated goal than Pompeii.

Nevertheless, the tourist industry, which in its distant medieval
origins seems to be mixed up with the religious custom of pilgrim-
ages (the first "tourist guide" to Rome is the eighth-century

*58, 59. Two drawings of Rome from Goethe's* Travels in Italy *(1816-17). Above, the Villa Medici. Below, the Pyramid of Gaius Cestius.*

*Itinerarium* of the Benedictine Abbey of Einsiedeln in Switzerland), arose at the beginning of modern times out of an urge felt by cultivated Europeans to know the places once occupied by classical civilization, whose spirit they sought to evoke among the august ruins. From the time of the Renaissance, scholars, artists, and wealthy amateurs came to Rome, wrote accounts of their travels, made pictorial records of their impressions (as in the famous sketchbooks of the Dutch painter Martin van Heemskerk). The Goethe of *Travels in Italy* is typical of these pilgrims to the classical world. For the Nordic peoples the "land of sunshine" had a special attraction which continued into the nineteenth century, arrayed in romantic hues. Meanwhile, Greece and the East, explored at first only by isolated merchants and adventurers, had also opened their doors to a constantly increasing stream of visitors lured by the fascination of the monuments and the discovery of fabulous ancient cities. *Fin-de-siècle*

*60. The nocturnal spectacles of* Son et Lumière *(Sound and Light) are now also presented at archaeological sites. This photograph shows a performance in the Roman Forum.*

Egypt had already become a fashionable winter resort for European and American nabobs. Finally, today, after so many changes of taste in the arts, the general mass of travelers, understandably weary of the conventional and standardized tourist attractions, are also beginning to turn more and more toward the archaeological centers. Greece is becoming a serious rival of the Western European countries. The temples of Magna Graecia and Sicily, as well as the Etruscan burial grounds, are already proving as big a draw as the art treasures of Venice, Florence, or Siena.

The tourist industry is not only a cultural factor; it is also an important economic one. The advent of foreign visitors represents, in all circumstances and from every aspect, a source of development and wealth for the places visited, an inexhaustible income for the countries with the greatest influx of guests from beyond their frontiers. For example, it is reckoned that the tourist industry currently contributes more than one and one-half billion dollars a year to the Italian economy. The increment is steadily increasing: in the ten years from 1956 to 1966 the number of foreign visitors to Italy more than doubled, increasing from about 12,500,000 to about 26,643,000 per annum. Archaeological and artistic treasures constitute one of the most valuable and profitable "raw materials" Italy possesses. This

COLORPLATE VII. *The Greek theater at Epidaurus, built by Polyclitus the Younger in the fourth century* B.C., *is still today a famous center of classical drama.*

fact should be constantly borne in mind by the authorities and by public opinion. In order to show these treasures to the best advantage, grants should be allocated in proportion to their importance, calculated on a simple economic basis quite apart from ideal and cultural reasons. In fact, this consideration meets with stubborn incomprehension (and not only in Italy), as demonstrated by the ludicrously small sums set aside in national budgets, and the consequent continual deterioration of these irreplaceable possessions.

Of course, when we speak of the profits deriving from the monumental patrimony of a country, this does not mean simply the direct benefits of admission charges to monuments or museums, or copyright fees for photographic reproductions, and the like. These comparatively modest revenues (in which the financial administration of the State seems to show an exaggerated, not to say anachronistic, interest) are not really even remotely commensurate with the great influx of indirect contributions from the tourist industry on a national level. It could even be argued that to charge entrance fees for visiting publicly owned art treasures (apart from any moral and cultural considerations) conflicts with the requirements of large-scale tourist traffic. Such charges have been abolished in a number of countries, and where they survive (as in Italy) so many categories of visitors qualify for free admission — students, certain groups of tourists, school children, etc. — that it would be easy, as well as desirable, to abolish this toll altogether. One can also point out the disadvantage to the tourist industry of the restricted opening hours of museums, groups of monuments, and excavations, especially on summer afternoons, not to mention the practice of closing them on a certain day of the week. On the other hand, the custom now being introduced of opening museums periodically for evening visitors seems an excellent one. As regards facilities for drawing, photographing, and filming monuments and works of art, these are being continually extended in civilized countries; and it is to be hoped that the right to make and freely circulate reproductions of works of art (which, it should be repeated, are the patrimony of all) will be recognized and universally admitted with the least possible delay, as opposed to the monopolistic speculation of private archives and photographers, and the restrictions of niggardly public administrations.

The pleasant arrangement of monumental and archaeological sites, the work of restoration, and the method of displaying museum collections, all play an important part in enabling the various countries to derive the maximum benefit from the tourist industry in respect to their own historical and artistic patrimony. Enormous advances have been made in this field in a very short time, particularly since the end of World War II. Gone are the days when the romantic ruin was all the vogue. Excavations and ancient monuments, if they are not to remain an impenetrable confusion of illegible stones or deteriorate into heaps of rubble, must be consolidated and organized, made easily accessible, laid out with trees, repaired, and even dis-

61, 62. Until the beginning of this century tourism was predominantly individual, and travelers were often art lovers and collectors. Above, King Ludwig I of Bavaria. Below, J. Pierpont Morgan in Egypt in 1909. Photo courtesy of the Trustees of the Pierpont Morgan Library, New York.

100

63-65. *In our own time mass travel has gradually taken the place of individual travel, as seen here in the crowds visiting the sights of Rome.*

*66. This bronze putto by Donatello, executed c. 1440, derives from classical models. National Museum (Bargello), Florence.*

creetly reconstructed, so that they can be enjoyed and understood by the maximum number of visitors with the widest possible range of cultural backgrounds. Italy is familiar with both early and very recent experiments in this field, models of their kind, from Pompeii and Herculaneum to the necropolis of Cerveteri, from the sanctuary of Palestrina to Hadrian's Villa at Tivoli and the villa of Piazza Armerina in Sicily. The same can be said of the museums, whose style of display, with plentiful explanatory material, is designed to take into account the level of knowledge of the average tourist.

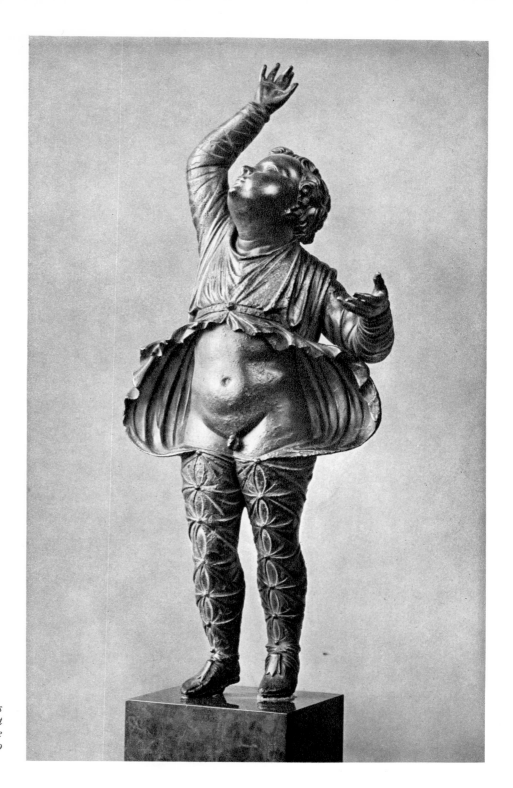

67. *Roman bronze statuette of Attis in the Louvre. The head and right hand are later restorations. Compare this example with the Donatello putto on the opposite page.*

But this is not all. In some cases ancient monuments can be given new life if suitable use is made of them, such as the performance of classical (and modern) plays given in Greek and Roman theaters. In recent years these have created a whole new tradition of dramatic art, evocative or experimental, which is evidently becoming more and more firmly established and widespread, and whose literary researches and style of production have not been without influence on the contemporary theater in general. The performances in the theaters of Epidaurus, of Herodes Atticus in Athens, of Syracuse and Ostia have

68. Detail of a ceiling painted by Perino del Vaga in Castel Sant'Angelo, Rome (1542-45). This kind of decoration took its name "grotesque" from paintings of the sort found in the Domus Aurea of Nero (the "grotto") at the end of the fifteenth century.

69. The Farnese Cup, a large sardonyx cameo depicting the fertility of the Nile, made in Alexandria in Hellenistic times. It passed from Lorenzo de' Medici to Pope Paul II and thus became part of the Farnese Collection, now in the National Museum, Naples. Its influence upon decorative taste from the Renaissance onward was considerable.

70. Signed copy of the Laocoön by Baccio Bandinelli. Uffizi Gallery, Florence.

104

71. *Stage design, drawing by Giovanni Maria Galli, known as Il Bibiena. Department of Drawings and Prints, Uffizi Gallery, Florence.*

72. *The Villa Rotonda in Vicenza, by A. Palladio and V. Scamozzi, was begun in 1550. Palladio's architecture expressed the classical spirit in a particularly appealing manner.*

become famous throughout the world. By bringing these monuments to light, archaeology can claim to have contributed to a far wider knowledge of the works of Aeschylus, Sophocles, Euripides, Aristophanes, and Plautus than could ever have been thought possible with books and schools. Open-air opera, too, has found impressive classical settings in the Baths of Caracalla in Rome and the amphitheater in Verona. Recently, more popular (and perhaps slightly commonplace) ways of summoning up the past have been created among the ancient monuments, such as the *son et lumière* spectacles.

Linked with the existence and growth of the tourist industry are advertising, organized travel, the hotel trade, the activities of guides, illustrated guidebooks and brochures, together with, on a lower level, the whole picturesque world of casual hangers-on: souvenir and curio sellers, cab drivers, renters of rooms, innkeepers, refreshment-stall proprietors, who congregate in tiresome swarms at some of the famous archaeological sites in the Mediterranean countries, but who, in the face of the new collective forms of the "grand tour," are tending gradually to disappear, along with the individualistic figure of the English traveler so characteristic of the nineteenth century.

73. *The Teatro Olimpico, Vicenza, by Palladio. It is believed to have been executed by Scamozzi or by Palladio's son, Silla. Begun in 1580, it was completed in 1585.*

## Archaeology as an influence on taste

Nowadays the enthusiasm for archaeology takes on a character somewhere between the intellectually oriented and the fashionable, particularly in circles which aspire to originality. We can see artists deriving ideas from prehistoric, archaic, or Etruscan discoveries — Picasso, for instance, in the "Mediterranean myths" of the Antibes paintings, the Vallauris ceramics, and the drawings. This seems, however, to be no more than a passing episode. Usually, imitation of the antique remains confined to the work of humble local artisans, particularly active around archaeological sites, and is produced for tourist consumption — jewelry, ceramics, printed fabrics, etc. In spite of the success of these themes in publishing, in the periodical press, on television, and in exhibitions, outside the field of scholars and the more serious amateurs and collectors these activities tend, like the craze for archaeology itself, to become a kind of fashionable exhibitionism, the idle *divertissement* of would-be intellectuals — in other words, an outside factor which does not impinge on culture, and which, far from representing a genuine original motive, often lapses into the commonplace.

74, 75. In his prints, G. B. Piranesi (1707-1778) brought out the picturesque and exotic aspects of the antique. Above, a fireplace with Egyptian decoration. Below, an engraving of the Temple of Ceres at Paestum; it emphasizes the grandeur of the ruins.

110

76, 77. *Neoclassical taste. Above, a late eighteenth-century English chest, its decoration inspired by Wedgwood porcelain. Below, a typical Empire-style dining room in the royal villa of Marlia, Lucca.*

78-80. *The following examples of the Three Graces show how classical themes continued to inspire artists from the Renaissance until the Neoclassical period. Above, Hellenistic-Roman wall painting from the house of T. Dentati at Pompeii. National Museum, Naples. Below, detail of a fresco by Francesco del Cossa in the Palazzo Schifanoia, Ferrara (1469-70). Opposite, group by A. Canova: the marble version is in the Hermitage, Leningrad; this photograph is of the plaster.*

ON PAGE 114

81, 82. *Classical dress of the French Revolution and the Empire. Above, satirical print against Barras, 1798: "The Parisian Sultan or the Embarras de Richesses." Below, Madame Récamier, by Jacques-Louis David. 1800. The Louvre, Paris.*

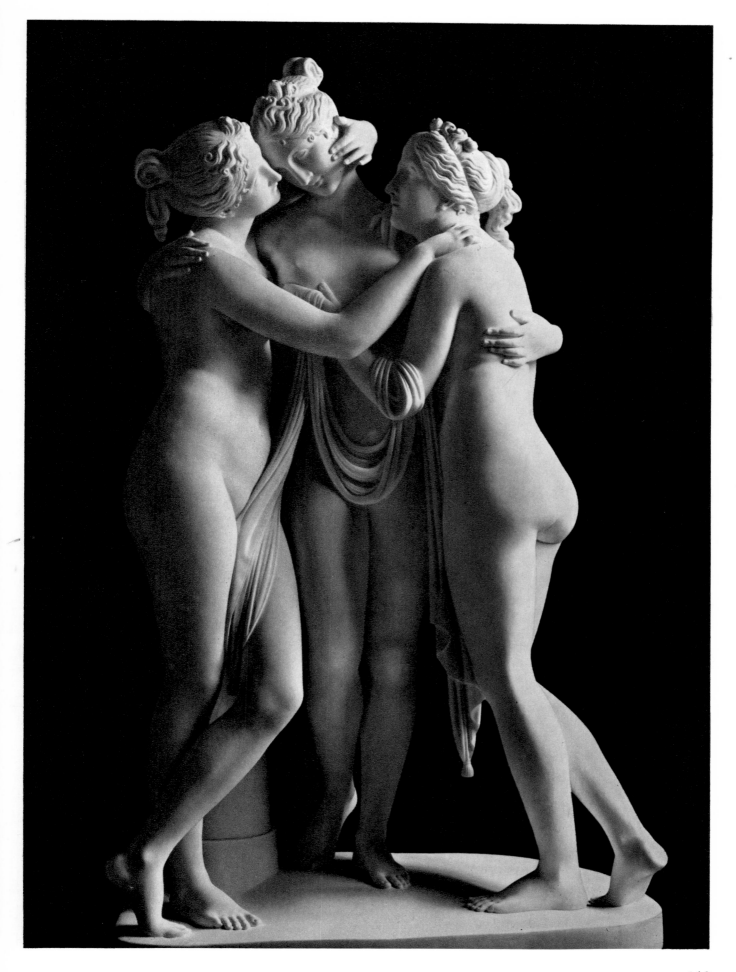

COLORPLATE VIII. *The Rape of the Sabines, by Jacques-Louis David (1748-1825). The inspiration for this famous painting had come to the artist during his stay in Rome. Its subject matter and sculptural forms illustrate very clearly the extent to which Neoclassical art drew upon ancient sources. David became Napoleon's court painter. The painting, completed in 1799, is now in the Louvre.*

Very different, and much more profound, has been the influence of archaeology on the tastes of society in other periods. It could even be said that, before becoming defined as a scientific discipline, it constituted an essential element of culture seen as a whole, including its most vital aspects of creativity and custom. It is difficult to determine, in the field of Renaissance classicism, how much the study and admiration of antique monuments and actual archaeological activities drew inspiration from the historico-literary and philosophical ideals of humanism; and, conversely, how much — not as effect but as cause — they were a decisive factor in the formation of Italian and European civilization in the fifteenth and sixteenth centuries. Unquestionably, many aspects of Renaissance art and thought derive directly from the antique tradition, rediscovered and revived, from the writings of Plato or Vitruvius. But the programs and experiments of the great architects and town planners of that period, from Leon Battista Alberti and Nicholas V to Bramante, Antonio da Sangallo, and Palladio, as well as the work of the great painters and sculptors, and often that of the poets themselves — indeed, the whole spirit and form of Renaissance decoration, fantasy, and symbolism — would be inconceivable without the immediate influence of the classical models emerging from the earth, the remains of buildings, frescoes, statues, coins, and gems lovingly observed and collected. It can in fact be said that the antique object has never

*83, 84. The Danish sculptor B. Thorvaldsen (1779-1844), trained in Canova's Roman circle, passionately and faithfully absorbed the ideals of classical art. He was also one of the initiators of the new archaeology of the early nineteenth century. Left, replica of the Apollo Sauroctonos by Praxiteles in the Vatican Museum. Right, Thorvaldsen's delicate statue of Adonis, inspired by the work of Praxiteles. Bayerische Staatsgemäldesammlungen, Munich.*

had such a direct and simple, yet at the same time such a profound influence as it did then, not only on figurative culture, but also on the current production which sets its stamp on the style and mentality of a period. Thus classical civilization seems to have continued and developed into modern civilization, rather than to have been revived after a gap of centuries.

Nevertheless, the Renaissance belongs of course to the modern and not the ancient world, as can be seen from Europe's progressive experience of the Reformation and the Counter Reformation, and later of absolutism and the Enlightenment. Although in the seventeenth and eighteenth centuries, as already said, the study of antiquities gradually lost the ideal motives which had permeated humanistic society, and withdrew into the sphere of scholarship, this does not mean that the Baroque eighteenth century, for example, did not continue to draw constant inspiration from antique models in decorative sculpture, furniture, costume, and jewelry, or that the monarchs of that period did not have their portraits painted armed and cloaked in the style of the statues of Roman emperors. But in much of this there is already a flavor of a masquerade — something external and artificial which seems far removed from the lively, sincere,

*85-87. Opposite, exterior and interior views of the Temple of Possagno, at the birthplace of A. Canova (1757-1822). It was built by the artist and houses his tomb. It is a free interpretation of the Pantheon in Rome. Below, interior view of the Pantheon, Rome.*

ON PAGE 120

*88, 89. Typical examples of the Greek revival in Germany. Above, the Walhalla or Pantheon of the Heroes by Leo von Klenze, near Regensburg, built at the instigation of Ludwig I of Bavaria and modeled on the Parthenon. 1831-42. Below, Von Klenze's Propylaea of the Royal Palace in Munich, 1846-63.*

COLORPLATE IX. *Early nineteenth-century Neoclassical bath in the Royal Palace at Caserta.*

90, 91. *Art Nouveau. Above, design for a wall by the Czech architect Jan Kotera (1871-1923). Below, sitting room-studio of the architect G. Monti (active c. 1900).*

spontaneous synthesis of ancient and modern which was characteristic of the Renaissance. In fact, seventeenth- and eighteenth-century classicism, no longer in such close contact with archaeological sources, is to be regarded rather as a trend that expresses the literary and philosophical principles of rationalism as opposed to the naturalistic and fantastic aspirations of Baroque and Rococo.

Archaeology, on the other hand, was given fresh impetus by the resurrection of Herculaneum and Pompeii and the awakening of European interest in the monuments of the East. Toward the middle of the eighteenth century it again offered food for curiosity and stylistic inspiration to a society singularly well prepared to receive them, both through excess of culture and doctrine and through restlessness of spirit. This time, however, it offered these, as it were, from the outside, as a discovery on the intellectual level, a recalling of the past, almost a nostalgia for it, or a taste for the exotic. In the majestic visual poetry of G. B. Piranesi's engravings, the subjects taken from the classical monuments appear transfigured by an imagination which extracts from them, and sublimates, the feeling for the gigantic, for antiquity, for ancient ruins; and alongside the classical themes, Etruscan and Egyptian motives make their appearance.

*92, 93. Left, runic stele. Right, government offices in Oslo; the mural decoration is inspired by runic stones.*

94, 95. Above, the Mausoleum of Ataturk in Ankara. Below, the Central
Library of the University of Mexico,
designed by J. O'Gorman, G. Saave-
dra, and Juan Martinez de Velasco.
1951-53. The decoration of the façade
derives from Pre-Columbian art.

*96. The hydraulic works at Philadelphia, on the Schuylkill River, probably designed by Robert Mills and begun in 1811. In the background, the Philadelphia Museum of Art, designed by Horace Trumbauer and others. Begun in 1919 and opened in 1928.*

Originating in Rome, the influence of the antique permeated the whole of European culture in the course of a few decades, creating that Neoclassical movement, so full of variety and contradictions and so difficult to define, which is a combination of theory, style, political ideology, customs, and mentality. The work of the archaeologists, or of the art and architectural theorists, such as Gotthold Ephraim Lessing, Sir Joshua Reynolds, Francesco Milizia, Luigi Lanzi, and

Ennio Quirino Visconti, as well as that of Winckelmann himself, is inextricably interwoven with that of the artists, painters, and sculptors from Mengs to Jacques-Louis David, Canova, and Thorvaldsen, the architects and decorators such as Robert Adam, Jacques-Ange Gabriel, Karl Schinkel, and the like. Direct echoes of Pompeian paintings, Roman stuccoes, Etruscan vases are to be found assembled in the matchless English interiors of the late eighteenth century, in

the ceramic ware of Josiah Wedgwood, and in Empire style furniture. Even women's fashions (a case unique in the history of antique influence on the modern world) adopted a severe classical line. After the arrival of the Elgin Marbles in Europe, Neoclassicism became more and more colored by Greek influence, no longer received via Rome, but gathered from the fresh enchantment of the Hellenic originals. It was spoken of as a Greek revival; the stern Doric architecture seemed particularly congenial to early nineteenth-century Germany.

There is no doubt that archaeology experienced its most definite and significant cultural expansion during the Neoclassical period. It found a response in a taste often of great refinement, in an ordered decorative sense, in mature and delicate techniques. Nevertheless, the movement clearly remained conditioned by its essentially learned origins. Thus, in the political usage and classicizing symbolism exalted by the French Revolution and the reign of Napoleon, as in the attempt to translate these ideals into high art, one can clearly see the imprint of an external inspiration, chilly and pompous — almost a pose or a disguise. Later, in the course of the nineteenth century, imitations of the antique became less and less consistent with the

*97, 98. Archaeological influence on the stage. Below, scene from the first production of* La Città Morta *by Gabriele d'Annunzio at the Théâtre de la Renaissance, Paris, in 1898. Although somewhat eclectic, the scenery is recognizably more derivative of the Greek classical period than "Mycenaean." Opposite, the Carthaginian setting for the Italian film* Cabiria, *1913, containing both Oriental and imaginary elements.*

128

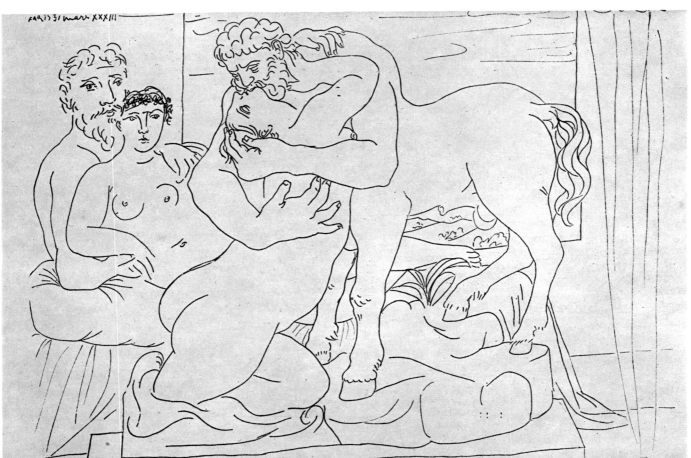

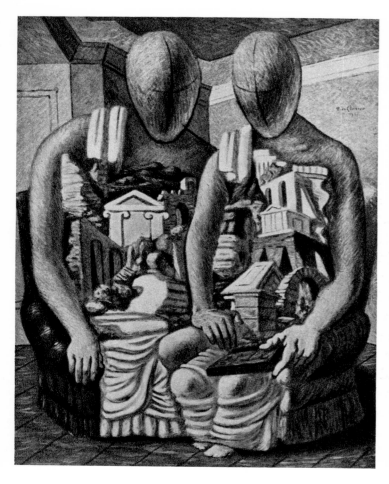

99-102. *Contemporary art with classical inspiration. Opposite page above, drawing of ruins on Paros by Ben Nicholson, 1959. Opposite page below, drawing by Pablo Picasso, 1931. Above, Giorgio de Chirico: The Archaeologist. Right, Salvador Dali: The Venus de Milo with Drawers, 1936.*

developments of contemporary culture, lapsing into collections of decorative formulas, architectural and furnishing pastiches, or ponderous manifestations of erudite pedantry (for instance, the museums built in various styles, from the Gregoriano Egizio of the Vatican to the Ny Carlsberg Museum in Copenhagen), Romantic outdoor settings of imitation ruins, or appalling "archaeological" and exotic fantasies such as the now demolished Pennsylvania Station in New York, copied from the Baths of Caracalla, or, in our own day, Mexico City University.

Finally, one must not omit the relationship between archaeology and the drama. The influence of ancient monuments and the desire to be as faithful as possible to models from antiquity was already evident in the scenic apparatus of Renaissance festivals and drama, which often derived their themes as well from classical sources. (In this respect, incidentally, they resembled the other aspects of the taste of that age.) In reality, it was mainly a question of an interpretation of the antique adapted to the contemporary spirit, all the more appreciable in such fields as dramatic action or choreography, just as, later, these had a Baroque, a Neoclassical, or a Romantic interpretation. Obviously, the realistic inclinations of the nineteenth century and the progress of archaeological discoveries were bound to set a problem of "reconstructive" objectivity and exactness in the setting and costumes for representations of historical subjects. Yet the modern theater, at its most effective, has turned more and more in the opposite direction of fantastic or symbolic suggestion, which deliberately rejects the preoccupation with faithful reproduction of setting, turning to archaeology only, if at all, for a few isolated allusive elements. Of course, this is not true of the cinema, which, being essentially visual narrative, calls for authenticity in its settings. It cannot, in fact, be imagined without a concrete reconstruction of the architecture, furnishings, costumes, ornaments belonging to the time and place of the action, and made possible only by the direct study of the original monuments, representations, and objects. Historico-archaeological documentation conditions the very bearing, gestures, and actions of the characters, and even limits the content of the sequences shot. For example, a certain ceremony or a certain method of fighting can be introduced only in a narrative which belongs to its period or civilization, and not anywhere else. Nevertheless, with rare exceptions, these requirements are not yet felt to be an essential element of the artistic value of a film on a historical subject, particularly in the case of films set in antiquity. (For more recent periods, there have been some magnificent efforts by the English, Russian, and Italian cinema.) Not only in ordinary productions, but also in the "epic" films on Biblical, Greek, or Roman themes, archaeological data are used in a superficial, vulgar, and arbitrary fashion, at an extremely low level of taste, and often limited to a few conventional motives of proved spectacular effect (parades, banquets, dances, battles) according to the demands of the market.

# THE GREAT ARCHAEOLOGICAL THEMES

### Archaeology as the history of antique art

The fortunes of the Laocoön, a Greek work preserved in the heart of Imperial Rome, can justly be claimed to symbolize the heroic phase of archaeology and its discovery of classical art. This piece of sculpture came to light, prophetically, at the height of the Renaissance. It immediately became famous, and was reproduced in the work of many artists. Michelangelo admired it. On various occasions it was restored (from the traditional sixteenth-century repair work of Giovannangelo Montorsoli and Michelangelo himself to the present-day definitive restoration by Filippo Magi and Antonio Berti). For centuries it has been regarded as a model, not only of antique sculpture, but even of sculpture in the absolute sense, and has been the subject of innumerable studies and discussions.

On the subject of the Laocoön, it must of course be pointed out that our own generation and age have been singularly privileged to witness the discovery of the marble fragments of a magnificent complex of groups and statues in the "grotto of Tiberius," on the Sperlonga coast between Rome and Naples. These include representations of Ulysses' ship and Scylla, which can be identified as further original works by Athenodorus, Agesander, and Polydorus, artists of the Hellenistic period from Rhodes, who were stated by Pliny (*Naturalis Historia*, XXXVI, 37) to be the sculptors of the Laocoön itself. This is revealed not only by the style and technique but also by the presence of an inscription recording the names of these artists. The new discovery makes it possible for historians of antique art to throw a brilliant and unexpected light on a particularly celebrated piece of sculpture, which today seems with more and more justification to be ranked among the great and exuberant creations, full of movement and pathos, of Hellenistic art in Asia Minor in the second century B.C.

The classical ideal of the Laocoön is really only one aspect, therefore, and a relatively late one, of the manifestations of Greek figurative genius. Obviously, it cannot be taken as the very model of perfection, as it was by artists and writers of treatises during the Renaissance; but neither do we any longer agree with the negative judgments of art historians of the generation immediately preceding our own, when this group was classified as a work of decadence, full of anatomical and psychological virtuosity rather than of poetry. Instead, we recognize its genuine artistic worth — particularly since the close examination of the individual sculptured parts, as a result of its recent restoration.

In truth, almost up to the threshold of the last century, knowledge of classical art was based essentially on works of the Hellenistic and Roman period — in other words, on relatively humble copies or elaborations of anonymous works, or on decorative sculpture and painting. Before Winckelmann there was a complete lack of any kind of historical perspective. To him alone, that rich and most lucid mind, must go the credit for having sought, in contrast to the pedantic or fanciful mythological interpretations of figurative subjects proposed by his learned contemporaries, what he called the nature or essence of the work of art (that is to say, its form and style), and for having distinguished between the pre-eminent creative role of Greece, mistress of classicism, and the developments and the imitations of the Roman period. Instinctively sensing a succession and an evolution of styles, he opened the way to the identification, through copies made in the Roman period, of famous works by Greek sculptors recorded in the literary sources. This work was carried out mainly by Italian archaeologists, such as Fea, who recognized the Discobolus of Miron, and Ennio Quirino Visconti, who identified the Cnidian Aphrodite of Praxiteles. In the meantime, the art of the Egyptians and the Etruscans had also found a place among the lines of development of ancient art as a whole; but whereas the priority of the first in relation to Greece and Rome was unchallenged, only Lanzi succeeded in demonstrating, in opposition to the still somewhat nebulous ideas of Winckelmann himself, the dependence of Etruscan art on that of Greece.

It seems incredible that Winckelmann should have perceived the basic outlines of the history of the antique world's artistic culture without having known the original masterpieces of Greece. Indeed, it was only some years after his death in 1768 that the sculptures from the Parthenon, brought back to Europe by Lord Elgin, became known and that their superb quality was appreciated — particularly by Canova and Visconti, who rightly saw in them the exemplary prototypes of classical art at the peak of its creative process, that is, in the third quarter of the fifth century B.C., under the inspiration of Phidias' genius. In 1811 the sculptures from the pediments of the Temple of Aegina came to light. These were immediately snapped up for the newly developing Munich sculpture gallery by the enlightened hereditary prince (later king) Ludwig of Bavaria. They pro-

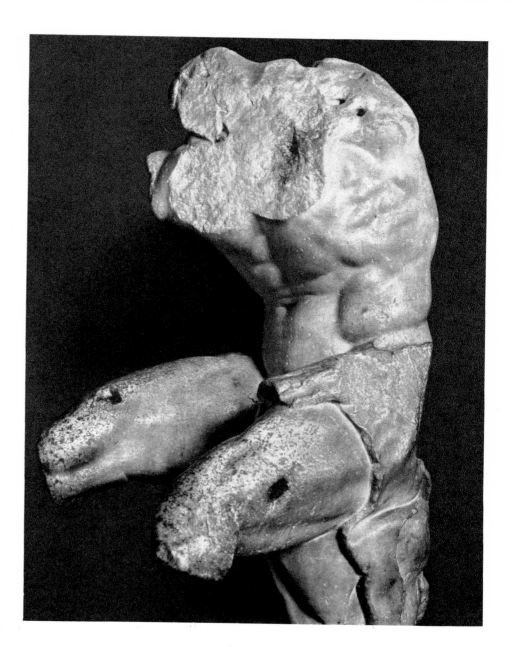

*103. The Belvedere Torso in the Vatican. Like the Laocoön, it dates from the Hellenistic period; it is one of the mighty symbols of the resurrection of ancient art during the Renaissance. Signed by the Athenian sculptor Apollonius, son of Nestor.*

vided the first glimpse of the world of Greek archaic art. Meanwhile, discoveries of painted pottery, particularly in the cemeteries of Etruria, became more and more frequent. Lanzi recognized these to be Greek products, in spite of their designation as Etruscan vases, and they provided a wealth of documentation on the development of Hellenic drawing and painting of the minor schools from the seventh to the fourth century B.C., which was assembled and elucidated by E. Gerhard.

In this way was born, at the dawn of the nineteenth century, the concept of archaeology as the history of antique art, or archaeology of art (*Archäologie der Kunst, Kunstarchäologie*). This concept, enshrined in a famous manual by K. O. Müller published in 1830, was to characterize the main trend of studies throughout the century, particularly where German scholarship was concerned. Archaeological investigations seemed to be entirely concentrated on the art of antiquity, its discovery and reconstruction — which meant in practice the classical

*104, 105. To the archaeologists of the nineteenth century, the development of Greek art began with the monuments of the Homeric age. Left, the Lion Gate at Mycenae, fourteenth century B.C. Right, huge geometric funeral vase depicting a funeral procession. From the Dipylon Cemetery in Athens. Eighth century B.C. National Museum, Athens.*

art of the Greeks and Romans. In this respect it appeared to be still tied to its humanistic origins, the wish to recover the antique forms which had spurred on the Renaissance artists searching among the ruins of Rome. As regards mentality and critical appraisal, too, the archaeology of art has never been able to forget the classicistic premises of the age in which it was born. The different movements which followed one another in the nineteenth century only succeeded in reinforcing, each in its own way, the influence of the "classical myth." Romanticism surrounded the image of ancient Greece with an aura of aesthetic mysticism; Positivism reinforced the principle of a closed evolutionary cycle which, starting from the beginning of Greek art, passed through its archaic youth, its classical maturity, its Hellenistic and Roman decadence, and finished with the end of the ancient world (linking this process with the technical conquest of true naturalism in anatomy and perspective, as explained so well by E. Loewy at the close of the nineteenth century).

Clearly, the identification and excavation of the most famous places in the Greek and Roman world, of which we have already spoken, were greatly encouraged by such ideas and theories. So also was the work of salvaging, classifying, interpreting, and studying ancient monuments and works of art. This fruitful activity in all its many

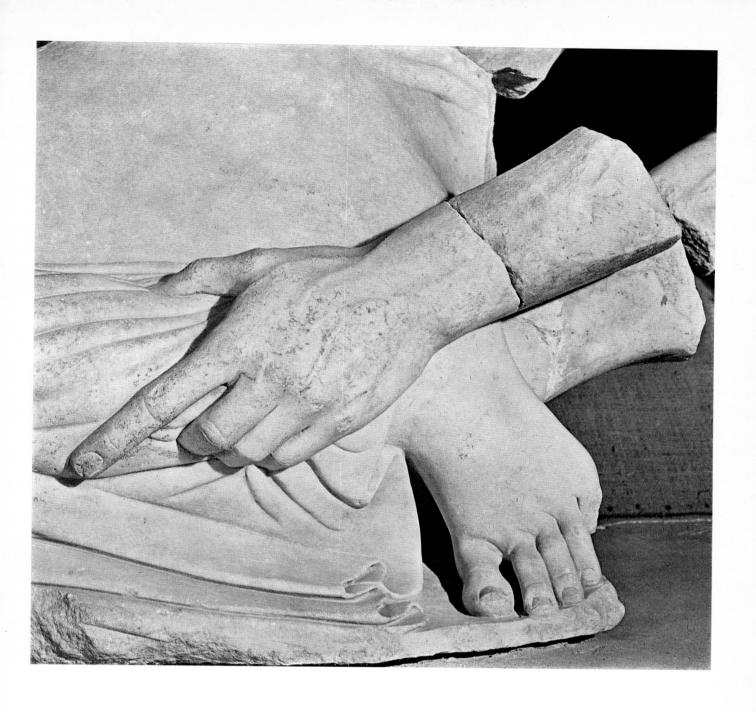

COLORPLATE X. *Detail of the battle between the Lapiths and the Centaurs from the west pediment of the Temple of Zeus at Olympia. In the details of the hands, feet, and drapery we see the beginnings of the harmony and force of the mature classical style. c. 460 B.C. Museum, Olympia.*

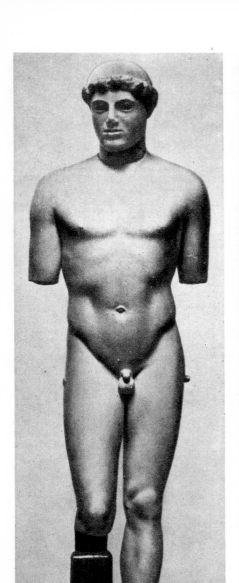

109, 110. The representation of the human figure in fifth-century classical Greece. Left, the Kritian Boy. c. 480 B.C. Acropolis Museum, Athens. Right, copy of the Athena Lemnia by Phidias. City Museum, Bologna.

even say, the mentality or "mystique" of its devotees — has met with an insuperable barrier to the understanding of historical reality as revealed by the discoveries made all around the frontiers of classicism, in the East and in the West, and in the periods immediately preceding and following the civilizations of Greece and Rome. Hence the general lack of interest among classicists in the artistic achievements of the ancient Near East, whose wealth of originality and superb aesthetic quality become more and more obvious, from the architectonic and figurative creations of pharaonic Egypt to the impressive works of the Sumerians, Babylonians, Hittites, Assyrians, the peoples of Iran and the Euro-Asiatic steppes, not to mention other more distant worlds. This conception of a "Greek miracle" concluded and brought to perfection within itself (in both its origins and its development) has resulted in the stubborn failure to comprehend the initial phenomena of Greek culture, and the phenomena related to it. In other words, this theory fails to find a logical posi-

111. *The three goddesses from the east pediment of the Parthenon by Phidias. c. 438-432 B.C. British Museum. The personal hand of the artist is particularly evident in the vitality and the subtlety of the flowing drapery, and in its contrast with the majesty of the figures.*

144

112, 113. *Following the Asiatic conquests of Alexander the Great a new concept of art, known as Hellenistic, grew up. This art was dynamic and realistic and emphasized contrasts of light and shade. Left, detail of the frieze on the Great Altar of Zeus at Pergamon. First half of the second century* B.C. *State Museums, Berlin. Above, Roman relief, incorporating elements of Hellenistic style, showing the Emperor Trajan fighting the Dacians. Beginning of the second century* A.D. *Parts of the relief were used again in the decoration of the Arch of Constantine in Rome.*

tion in the cycle of Greek art for the Aegean civilization of the second millennium, although it was so closely linked with historic Greece. According to evolutionist concepts, Greek art was born from the immature and primitive experiments of the geometric period, whereas these have been shown, on the contrary, to be in fact later than the splendid, mature creations of Mycenaean Crete. There is an additional difficulty in recognizing the historically original aspects of the peripheral artistic cultures of Asia Minor, Cyprus, the Scythians, Illyrians, Etruscans, Venetii, Celts, Iberians, etc. All this explains why the world of late antique, paleo-Christian, barbaric, and Byzantine art was abandoned to the care of historians of medieval art, as if through embarrassment at having to classify them *en bloc* as phenomena of decadence in relation to the ideals of classical art, which was how many great scholars were wont to regard them. This tremendous error in historical perspective was denounced by A. Riegl as early as the beginning of this century. Yet it was repeated again by that great art critic and historian Bernard Berenson, not long before his death.

These prejudiced attitudes have weighed heavily on the studies of the history of ancient art, and continue to do so. It is only in

147

quite recent years that a patient labor of revising the traditional framework has been in progress, on an archaeological basis and thanks essentially to archaeology. This is being achieved through a reassessment of classical Graeco-Roman civilization (de-mythicizing it, so to speak) against the background of the very complex and multiform sequence of inventions, traditions, customs, trends, and figurative influences which characterize the development of ancient humanity from prehistory to the Middle Ages. Only now are we beginning to perceive the fecundity of the artistic legacies of thousands of years of prehistory, to grasp the primary importance of the achievements of the Near Eastern countries beginning in the fourth millennium B. C., to understand that Greek art did not spring out of nothing but flowed like a great creative river from the contributions of the rivulets and main tributaries of Mediterranean and Eastern protohistory, to allot their proper place to the phenomena flourishing on the margins of the Greek world, with a partial influx

*114, 115. Ever since preclassical times artistic traditions of a somewhat primitive type flourished on the periphery of the Greek world. Left, detail of the Warrior of Capestrano, sixth century* B.C. *Chieti Museum. Right, terra-cotta statuette of a woman from Ibiza, one of the Balearic Isles. Fifth or sixth century* B.C. *Archaeological Museum, Madrid.*

COLORPLATE XI. *Golden death mask of a Mycenaean prince from Grave Circle A, Mycenae, between 1600 and 1500 B.C. National Museum, Athens. The discovery of the Minoan and Mycenaean civilizations during the last decade of the nineteenth century opened a new and unexpected chapter on the origins of Greek art.*

and development of Greek ideas, in Asia and Europe, and to recognize the artistic civilization of late antiquity as an important historical reality in its own right, no longer an integral part of the decadence of the ancient world or the infancy of the modern one.

## Monuments that "speak"

It is strange that the revelation of the ancient East, unlike the clearly delineated vision with which the classical world manifested itself, took place rather under the sign of its mysterious writings, almost like a message in a secret code. The ancients themselves must already have been fascinated by the Egyptian inscriptions, with their lively little figures of birds, animals, men, plants, and objects instead of letters, which they themselves called hieroglyphics, or "sacred carvings." And no doubt the decorated sides of the obelisks brought from distant Egypt to adorn the city of the Caesars were looked upon in the same way by the Romans of the Imperial epoch as they are by present-day sightseers — as incomprehensible oddities. In reality, it was these very obelisks raised by the Popes in the Roman squares which acted as the first messengers from Eastern civilization to humanistic Europe, and awakened that interest in Egyptian antiquities which was one of the features of seventeenth- and eighteenth-century erudition. But the learned Jesuit Kircher, like the ancient writers Plutarch and Horapollo, saw the hieroglyphs as arcane symbols of intricate mystical and religious doctrines; and he set to work to interpret them with the unbridled imagination characteristic of his time.

Even later, when the Napoleonic expedition brought Europeans into direct contact with Egypt and initiated the exploration of that fabulous land, it was still not the influence of the Pyramids and the other huge architectural and sculptured monuments which set its scientific and psychological imprint on the beginnings of Egyptology. It was once again the problem of the mysterious writing, and the urge to penetrate its secrets. As is well known, a happy chance decreed that in 1799, when the foundations of a French blockhouse were being dug at Rosetta, an inscribed stone was unearthed which was to become in a short time the center of world-wide interest, and was to provide the key to the history and civilization of Egypt and the whole of the ancient East. This relic, now housed with full honors in the British Museum, contains a decree of Ptolemy V, Epiphanes (205–182 B.C.), drawn up in three different scripts and three languages: Egyptian hieroglyphics, demotic script (the popular Egyptian writing of the Greek period), and Greek. This was the basic document which, after a series of vain attempts, led the young French philologist Jean-François Champollion to the decipherment of hieroglyphic writing and comprehension of the Egyptian language. In fact, it was recognized that the hieroglyphs were not purely ideogrammatic. The identification of phonetic signs in the

ON PAGE 151

*116. Detail of the large silver plate belonging to the Emperor Theodosius, late fourth century* A.D. *Royal Historical Academy, Madrid. The revision of traditional ideas about classical art reached a climax with the recognition of the definite artistic values of late antiquity.*

OPPOSITE

*117. Portrait of Champollion by Mme. Rumilly. Superimposed on the picture are phonetic signs included by Champollion in a letter to M. Dacier. From* Monuments et mémoires de la Fondation E. Piot.

Pl. IV.

# Tableau des Signes Phonétiques
## des écritures hiéroglyphique et Démotique des anciens Égyptiens

| Lettres Grecques | Signes Démotiques | Signes hiéroglyphiques |
|---|---|---|
| A | | |
| B | | |
| Γ | | |
| Δ | | |
| E | | |
| Z | | |
| H | | |
| Θ | | |
| I | | |
| K | | |
| Λ | | |
| M | | |
| N | | |
| Ξ | | |
| O | | |
| Π | | |
| P | | |
| Σ | | |
| T | | |
| Υ | | |
| Φ | | |
| Ψ | | |
| X | | |
| Ω | | |
| TO TA | | |

litho de Bernard rue de St Bernard N° 17

proper names of kings enclosed in an elongated ring (or royal cartouche) made it possible to read common words recognized as belonging to the Coptic language spoken in Egypt in the Byzantine and Arabic periods. Thus it was confirmed that Coptic was derived from the ancient national language of Egypt. With the help of this known language, the unknown hieroglyphic writing was interpreted, together with its cursive variants, hieratic and demotic. Champollion and his successors were thus able to begin the laborious task of translating the innumerable documents left behind by the ancient Egyptians in three thousand years of history.

Soon afterwards, a similar event occurred in connection with the writing of the peoples who had provided the other great beacon of civilization in the ancient East: the Sumerians, Babylonians, and Assyrians of Mesopotamia, and all the other Asiatic peoples who had adopted their system or forms of script — Hittites, Mitanni, the Syrians of Ugarit, Urartians, and Persians. This widely used writing, mentioned by Herodotus and first observed and copied by the Italian traveler Pietro della Valle at the beginning of the seventeenth century, was called cuneiform because of the wedge-shaped elements which made up the characters (*cuneus* = wedge). The great inscriptions of the Achaemenid kings, drawn up in Persian, Elamite, and

COLORPLATE XII. *Detail of the painting on a wooden Egyptian sarcophagus of the Middle Kingdom, c. 1850 B.C. Museum of Fine Arts, Boston. The minutely rendered hieroglyphs form part of the decorative scheme.*

Babylonian, provided a starting point for its decipherment, which was completed stage by stage in the first half of the nineteenth century by G. F. Grotefend, H. Rawlinson, I. Löwenstern, and E. Hinks. It began in much the same way as the decipherment of hieroglyphics — by the identification of proper names, the determination of the phonetic value of certain signs, and finally the recognition of linguistic structures known from other sources, such as Iranian (for the Persian texts) and Semitic (for the Babylonian texts). Later, once the secret of reading this graphic system had been penetrated, the knowledge was in turn used in the discovery and interpretation of hitherto unknown tongues such as Hittite.

The ability to make inscribed monuments "speak" is obviously a matter of the keenest interest for scholars investigating past civilizations. Such evidence could be said to combine the evocative power of the tangible object with that of speech itself. For this reason, from the time of the Renaissance the seekers of epigraphs (Latin, Greek, and Etruscan) were among the most dedicated of all antiquaries, and Greek and Latin epigraphy has since occupied a place in the forefront of the archaeological and historical disciplines. It is also true, however, that where these studies were concerned one was generally moving, in the West, over a territory which was culturally and linguistically familiar, and one had the support of the whole Graeco-Roman literary tradition. The East, on the other hand, was still a vast closed book, mysterious and fascinating. Moreover, those Oriental civilizations were seen to be composed, archaeologically, of obsessive writers mixing together words and pictures and covering hundreds upon hundreds of square yards of monumental walls with their texts, and leaving their records, thoughts, and comments everywhere upon steles, statues, tiles, textiles, papyri, and jewelry. This is why the study of Oriental antiquities — Egyptology, Assyriology, Hittitology, etc. — belonged primarily to the domain of philologists and linguists, rather than to that of pure archaeologists, and to a large extent still does. It also explains why, in the last analysis, there has been such a long delay in establishing a productive interchange of ideas, founded on a similar attitude and similar objectives, between classical and Oriental archaeology.

It is significant that the work of decipherment was generally sparked off by the discovery or study of bilingual (or trilingual) inscriptions. This shows that juggling with a combination of hypotheses, however ingenious, could never have led to absolute certainty without the external check of a "translation" based on the presence of known elements. Grotefend rightly stated, at the time of his first attempts with cuneiform writing, that "decipherment is impossible without some firm ground from which to start." This also applies to discoveries of minor importance or related to a culture more restricted in extent — such as the reading of the indigenous inscriptions of Lydia (achieved at the beginning of the present century with the help of a bilingual inscription in Lydian and Aramaic, and

120, 121. *Writing from the ancient Near East. Left, Assyrian cuneiform stele depicting Ashurbanipal as a basket bearer. Babylon, seventh century B.C. Right, hieroglyphic writing.*

two others, also bilingual, in Lydian and Greek) or the reading of the Cypriot inscriptions, which was aided by the discovery at Idalion of a fourth-century B.C. votive dedication to Apollo, in Cypriot and Phoenician. The decipherment of the African writing of the Numidians was also achieved principally by means of the great inscriptions of King Masinissa in Punic and Numidian. A particularly important case is that of the Hittite hieroglyphic writing, already in use in Asia Minor in the period of the great Hittite empire (in the second millennium B.C.), at the same time as the cuneiform writing, and later used more particularly in eastern Anatolia and northern Syria in a somewhat more recent epoch. This has the same pictorial character as the Egyptian hieroglyphs, but corresponds to an essentially syllabic system like that of the cuneiform script. Some progress had already been made in its decipherment on the strength of its affinity with the Hittite language transcribed in cuneiform (by F. Hrozný, P. Meriggi, I. J. Gelb, and others); but its definitive clarification and fullest confirmation once again had a bilingual basis, thanks to the sensational discovery made in 1946, at Karatepe in Cilicia, of a long historical double text in Hittite hieroglyphs and Phoenician.

The situation is very different when there is no *point d'appui*. Thus, in spite of endless attempts, solutions have yet to be found to the enigma of the so-called Sinaitic writing, the Cretan script known as Linear A, the fine isolated inscription stamped in a spiral on the two faces of a terra-cotta disk discovered at Phaistos, and the characters

122, 123. *Writing from the Aegean. Above, terra-cotta disk from Phaistos, Crete, inscribed in an unknown hieroglyphic script in a spiral on each side. After 1600 B.C. Archaeological Museum, Herakleion. Below, Mycenaean clay tablet inscribed with the Linear B script.*

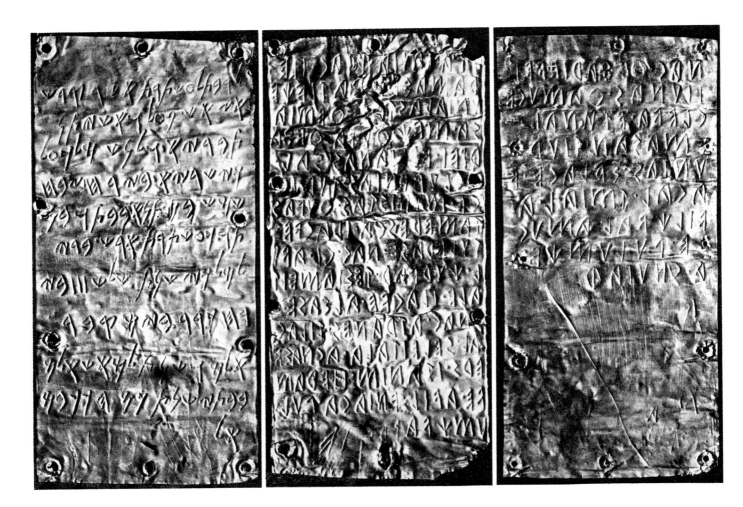

124-26. *Gold sheets with Phoenician (left) and Etruscan (center and right) inscriptions discovered in the Etruscan sanctuary of Pyrgi, the port of Cerveteri, early fifth century* B.C. *Villa Giulia Museum, Rome. The first and second documents have the same subject matter and can therefore be considered bilingual. These texts are of immense religious and historical significance because of the light they throw on relations between Etruscans and Carthaginians.*

on the seals and tablets of the Indus Valley civilization. The most hopeless cases are, of course, those in which an unknown writing is combined with an unknown language (and one which will presumably remain so). Of the indigenous pre-Roman writings of Spain, that of the eastern coast, the so-called Iberian, with its partly syllabic, partly alphabetic characters, has substantially been read by M. Gomez-Moreno, working on the basis of the ethnic names of the inscriptions on coins; but the longer texts on vases, tablets, and on stone are still only partly understood, and the writing of southern Spain, known as Tartessian, remains completely obscure.

The most recent puzzle of this kind, of absorbing interest and stirring news value, is the Mycenaean script known as Linear B. Vast quantities of texts on unbaked clay tablets discovered in the archives of the Palace of Knossos in Crete, in Pylos and Mycenae, and also on vases, are written in Linear B, which can be dated to the second half of the second millennium B.C. After long and fruitless endeavors, the Englishman Michael Ventris announced in 1953 that he had found the key to the syllabic characters of this writing, and that he could identify its language as Greek. Thus he confirmed the hypothesis, already advanced a number of times (and in itself a very probable one), that the people of the Mycenaean civilization, i. e., the Homeric Achaeans, were neither more nor less than the forebears of the Greeks of history — even the Greeks themselves in the first phase of their story. This was therefore a case of the deciphering of an unknown writing by means of a known language, as happened with the Egyptian hieroglyphs. Archaeologists, philologists, and linguists all over the world applied themselves enthusiastically to the task of developing and applying Ventris' system in every way to the reading and evaluation of the Mycenaean documents (unfortunately these seem to be mainly inventories of stores) — not without rash conjectures, uncertainties, contradictions, and even, on the part of some scholars, a certain amount of obstinate skepticism. This huge undertaking is still in progress. At the moment it would be premature to risk forecasting the final results; but it would obviously be of great value to discover at least one external *point d'appui*, in Grotefend's sense, in order to check the decipherment so far completed. Once again, we must pin our hopes on archaeology.

The problems concerning difficult, imperfectly known, or incomprehensible ancient languages of which we have some epigraphical evidence written in characters such as the Greek or Latin alphabet or a derivation of these, are really outside the scope of the present chapter. Certain inscriptions of the Aegean — to remain within the Mediterranean and European orbit — belong to this category, such as the famous stele of Lemnos or the Eteo-Cretan inscriptions of eastern Crete, in addition to many groups of inscriptions in the Alpine and Adriatic areas. Above all there is Etruscan, around the mystery of which has grown up what is by now a century-old atmosphere of myth and prejudice. All these matters belong more properly to the field of linguistic and historical studies rather than to archaeology. In fact, similar difficulties can be encountered in the reading of nonepigraphical documents handed down from literature. In any case, as far as Etruscan is concerned, it cannot be repeated too often that the understanding of the very few texts we possess does not depend on a miraculous key, as is popularly believed, but is the progressive result of a persistent work of philological analysis; and that the meaning of the greater part of the inscriptions and the essential features of the structure of the language have actually been known for a long time — in fact, from the beginning of Etruscological studies in the eighteenth century.

### The life of the past

Usually it is assumed that references to archaeological excavations imply the excavation of tombs. We have seen that for the ancient Greeks and Romans the knowledge of a buried past was already mainly identified with the reopening of ancient graves, though this was only an occasional or an illicit activity. From the point of view of the recovery of intact objects or groups of objects, for finding out about the background to life in ancient times, for the very survival of certain works of art, tombs provide archaeologists with absolutely unrivaled opportunities compared with other types of

127-29. *Ancient domestic interiors and their furnishings. Above, furniture from the tomb of Queen Hetepheres at Giza. Fourth Dynasty, c. 2600 B.C. Egyptian Museum, Cairo. Below, hall of the House of the Wooden Partition at Herculaneum, restored to its original appearance at the time of the eruption of Vesuvius in A.D. 79. Opposite, Room No. 8 of the House of the Charred Furniture, erected soon after the earthquake of A.D. 63.*

162

ON PAGE 164

*130. The Cave of the Cumaean Sibyl, on the acropolis of Cumae near Naples, is one of the most famous sanctuaries of antiquity. For religious reasons the Greeks excavated the gallery with its false vault, in imitation of the earliest tomb architecture.*

ON PAGE 165

*131. Entrance to the Tzarskii tomb near Kerch, the ancient Panticapaeum, in the Crimea. Fourth century B.C. The imposing tomb architecture with its false vaulting derives from traditional Mediterranean forms dating back to Mycenaean times.*

remains or other fields of research. Inhabited sites such as cities, fortresses, sanctuaries, or villas have inevitably suffered (except in very rare instances) during hundreds, even thousands, of years all the effects of transformation, decay, destruction, reoccupation, and rebuilding, in a continuous process through all the succeeding phases of their existence, so that monuments have been altered or destroyed and traces of human activity erased. The archaeological investigation of such sites, therefore, usually turns out to be a difficult and delicate operation, without very much in the way of sensational or immediate results. Tombs, on the other hand, were deliberately planned by the ancients as the inviolable dwellings of the dead: built, decorated, equipped, and sealed to provide a safe refuge from the depredations of men and of time. Thus they are fragments of the past set apart from the rhythm of life and preserved from the changes wrought by time, handed down to us as faithful mirrors of the civilizations of their own period.

The excavation of tombs brings us strangely close to the ancients as individuals and private citizens — their needs, their tastes, their habits. The pictures of domestic and social life, the feasts, the scenes of toil and recreation and of battles shown in reliefs and paintings in Egyptian and Etruscan sepulchers; the personal effects and household goods which accompanied the dead, the jewels and fabrics, the

163

132. *The Street of the Tombs, Pompeii. In classical times tombs often lined the roads leading out of towns. Mausoleums took the form of small temples or altars.*

shoes they wore (and here the evidence covers a geographical arc reaching from the Mediterranean to Pre-Columbian America, and thus makes contact with human civilization in the universal sense).

It should not be imagined, however, that burial grounds are our only source of data. There are other ways of coming into direct contact with a relatively intact past; the outstanding and in some ways unique example is the Campanian cities buried in the famous eruption of Vesuvius in A.D. 79 — Pompeii, Herculaneum, and Stabiae — a discovery of supreme importance for the whole history of archaeology. Here it was not the will of man but a tremendous natural catastrophe that was responsible for the cessation of life and the preservation of the antique complex through the ages. Here, crystallized forever in a single moment, is the complete world of these important centers of cultivated life, at the height of their activity, with the whole background of their urban development, their architecture, their decorative art forms both sophisticated and popular, their public life, their industries, trade, traffic, and entertainments; men and women of every social condition, encountered in their domestic intimacy or their daily intercourse in the streets and town squares. Were it not for the fact that we are to some extent accustomed to this prodigy, having been familiar with it for two centuries, we would never cease to marvel each time we visit Pompeii and Herculaneum, either in reality or in imagination.

Of course, a knowledge of the life of the ancient world is also obtained, even if in a less concrete form, from other discoveries and excavations. From the prehistoric caves and villages to the cities of the East, the Mediterranean, and Roman Europe, countless indications have been discovered, and are still coming to light, of the customs, economy, techniques, forms of association, human relationships, and the mentality of all the different peoples who have succeeded one another in those places, throughout the centuries, in every period and in all settings. Places of worship, in particular, temples and sanctuaries — where piety and conservatism often concealed consecrated objects and votive treasures — throw considerable light on religion, that central feature of all civilizations, with its beliefs, its divinities, its national and local traditions, its monuments, its forms of sacrifice and of prayer, its symbols and instruments. This is a field in which, because of the very quantity and the impressive nature of the evidence, largely composed of epigraphical documents (sacred texts, dedications, etc.), the archaeologist is easily tempted to become in-

volved, and to venture on the interpretation of his discoveries, thus turning into a historian of religions. It must be pointed out, however, that this is an extraordinarily difficult field, because one is dealing with the external reflections of a world of profound human experiences, of great complexity and by their very nature extremely difficult to understand. It is therefore all too easy to fall into error or indulge in flights of fancy.

Curiosity concerning the society and institutions of the past has for a long time remained on the margins of history, which has mainly concerned itself with great individuals and political and military events: in other words, the histories of Herodotus, Thucydides, Livy, and Tacitus. Now archaeological documentation has certainly contributed, step by step, to our knowledge of the main currents of external events, and even, in the case of some civilizations

*133-36. Above left, harp from a royal tomb at Ur. It is made of wood, bitumen, and strips of gold, and inlaid with lapis lazuli and shells. Height 55". Second half of the third millennium B.C. Reconstructed with the original fragments. University Museum, Philadelphia. Above right, toy box with gaming pieces from Abydos. Made of wood and faïence. Length 16". Fifteenth century B.C. Metropolitan Museum of Art, New York. Below left, Roman dish and small bronze instruments. Vatican Museum. Below right, articulated Roman doll from the tomb of the Vestal Cossinnia at Tivoli. Made of bone, second century A.D. National Museum, Rome.*

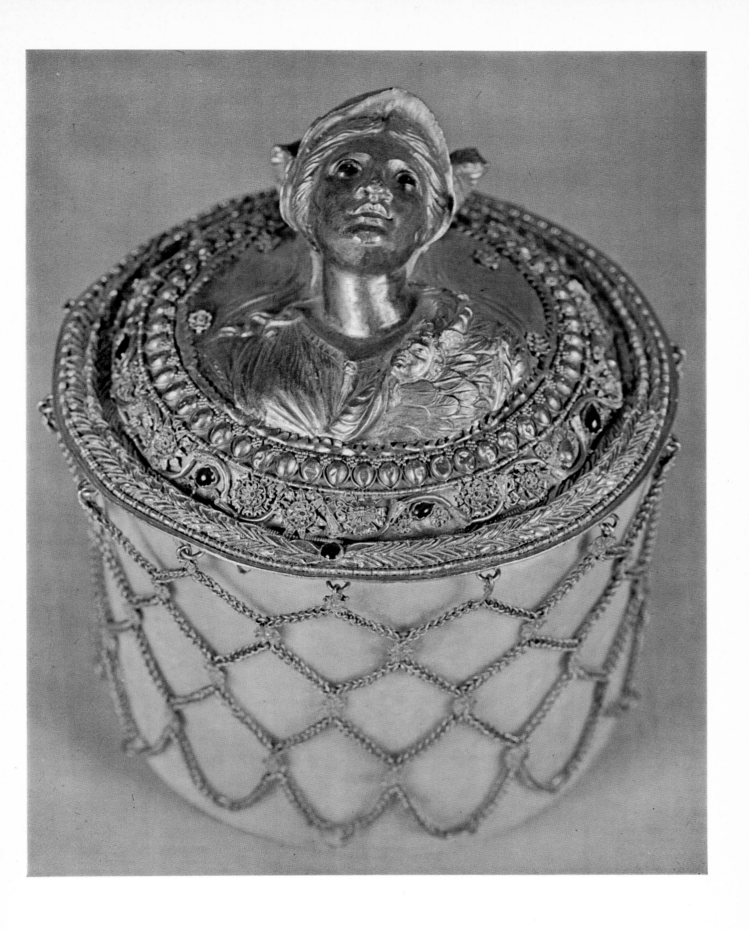

COLORPLATE XIII. *Gold medallion with bust of Athena, possibly a cover of a glass vase or of a cylindrical pyxis. From Thessaly, second half of the third century* B.C. *Benaki Museum, Athens.*

137, 138. *Above, the harps from Ur as they were discovered in 1922. Below, Egyptian furnishings and household implements from the Tomb of Kha in the necropolis of Thebes. Kha lived during the Eighteenth Dynasty, between the fifteenth and fourteenth centuries* B.C. *Egyptian Museum, Turin.*

139-41. *Representation of the daily life of the ancients in painting. Above, musicians and young Egyptian dancers from the tomb of Nakht in the necropolis of Thebes. c. 1400* B.C. *British Museum. Center, cooks and attendants at an Etruscan banquet, depicted on frescoes from the Golini Tomb at Orvieto. Fourth century* B.C. *Now in the Archaeological Museum, Florence. (From a watercolor reproduction.) Below, an enameler's workshop painted on a sarcophagus from southern Russia. First or second century* A.D. *The Hermitage, Leningrad.*

142-44. *Three details of mosaics.*
*Bardo Museum, Tunis.*

145. *Remains of the Roman baths at Timgad, dating from the Antonine period, second century* A.D.

174

146. Wall flanking the entrance to the shop of Marcus Vecilius Verecondus in the Via dell'Abbondanza, Pompeii. From top to bottom can be seen paintings of an election manifesto, the figure of Mercury leaving a small temple, and a scene at a cloth market.

147, 148. Reminders of public and private sufferings in votive reliefs. Below, a pious man cured of varicose veins offers a model of his own leg. Fourth century B.C. National Museum, Athens. Opposite, the earthquake of A.D. 63 at Pompeii as depicted on the base of the lararium in the house of Cecilius Giocondus.

such as those of the ancient Near East, has played a decisive part in the reconstruction of their story. But above all, archaeology brings to light aspects of history which are less obvious, though no less essential: its slow anonymous growth in remote periods before the existence of any written tradition, the demographic groupings and entities, the pressure of the masses, the economic conditions, the cultural levels and conflicts, the customs, and transformations, and daily activities. And it is this which constitutes its original and essential contribution to the reconstruction of ancient history.

Of course, as we already know, the concept of archaeology as the general reconstruction of the buried civilization of the past was only arrived at rather late in the day, and by gradual stages. An archaeologist from a Neoclassical courtly milieu — Ennio Quirino Visconti, for example — would never have visualized his successors gathering up and carefully studying the remains of a hearth, the pottery fragments in a tomb, the wooden structures of a building. (In those days all this evidence, so precious to us, was ignored and thrown aside as of no importance.) Only in the climate of the new Romantic and middle-class trends of the nineteenth century were the minds of men conditioned to approach the relics of the past — and history in general — with a predisposition to understanding and cherishing minor happenings, anonymous experiences, everyday life — with a taste for investigation which we could define as intimistic. Furthermore, at the end of the last century and the beginning of the present one the steady, progressive growth of interest in sociological and economic problems encouraged the study of antique monuments from the point of view of social structures, organization, production, and trade — an area of study which, as regards the classical world, and mainly on a basis of archaeological data, has been

*149, 150. Representations of the daily life of the ancients in sculpture. Above, payment of tribute money. Below, a school. These two reliefs come from the Roman province of Belgica and date from the second century A.D. Museum, Trier.*

most diligently and acutely explored by M. Rostovtzeff. Finally, in keeping with the interests of our own period, the analysis of man-made articles found by archaeologists is being extended to include the exact methods that were used, and the nature and provenance of the materials. This applies to architectural structures, objects carved in marble or in hard or soft stone, terra cottas, glassware, and especially metalwork; and, of course, to the investigation of the origins and history of the various processes, of inventions and improvements. The modern observer does not overlook the importance of the scientific and technical methods of antiquity, particularly in the Hellenistic and Roman periods — as revealed, for example, in the arrangements for collecting, channeling, and distributing water (which was often piped to private properties), in the drainage systems, the up-to-date warm-air heating installations, the fitting-out of ovens and workshops; in vehicles, in the design of ships (revealed especially by underwater archaeology in the sea and in the lake of Nemi); in various machinery for lifting, transporting, cutting, throwing (engines of war, for example), and weaving; and finally, all the instruments

COLORPLATE XIV. *Askos or vase in the shape of a wineskin, with relief decoration and the painted figure of a winged seahorse. Hellenistic period, from Canosa in Apulia. Archaeological Museum, Bari.*

151. Industry. Scene in a mine. Terra-cotta plaque from Corinth, fourth century B.C. State Museums, Berlin.

and apparatus, sometimes of great refinement, connected with the trades and professions of the architect, engineer, sculptor, joiner, goldsmith, dyer, tailor, shoemaker, surgeon, druggist, surveyor, astronomer, clerk, and teacher.

### "Sacred archaeology"

On 28 June 1939, soon after the accession of Pope Pius XII, a memorable piece of excavation was begun in the very heart of one of the most sacred places in Christendom — under the Vatican basilica — to search for the tomb of St. Peter.

This was not in fact the first time that archaeology had tackled problems connected with sacred subjects, or with the history of Judaism or Christianity. From the time of the great Renaissance exploration of the ruins of Rome, attention had been drawn to the

152, 153. *Industry. Left, partly reconstructed oil press in the Villa dei Misteri, Pompeii. Below, bronze tap from the water system for the Roman ships at Nemi. From a cast in the Museum of Roman Civilization, Rome.*

OPPOSITE

154. *Palace of Knossos, Crete. Magazine with huge terracotta vases used for storing provisions.*

ON PAGE 184

155. *Interior of a large food shop at Herculaneum.*

COLORPLATE XV. *A dog's collar and identity disk from Pompeii. National Museum, Rome.*

early Christian cemeteries or "catacombs" (derived from a medieval Greek designation for the cemetery of St. Sebastian *kata kymbas*, "near the ravines"). These were opened in great numbers all over the city, with their complicated and mysterious subterranean galleries, innumerable burial niches, sepulchral chambers, unsophisticated paintings and stone tablets. Above all, there was a reawakening of interest in the relics of the martyrs, alleged by medieval traditions, sometimes authentic and sometimes unfounded, to be buried in the large and small suburban basilicas and in the vaults of the catacombs. This line of investigation was very dear to the Counter Reformation, as can be seen from the boundless enthusiasm shown for it by Philip Neri, the Roman saint, and the fine work on the subject by Antonio Bosio, *Roma sotterranea*, published in 1632. It was continued during the following centuries, not without much destruction of monuments (some of it for pious ends!), and finally enjoyed a vigorous revival, in the direction of historical criticism, in the works of the Jesuit Giuseppe Marchi (1795–1860) and of Giovanni Battista De Rossi (1822–1894), founders of the discipline known as Christian archaeology.

Of course, the study of early Christian monuments quickly spread beyond Rome to the rest of Italy, continental Europe, Africa, and the East, and finally became identified with the civilizations of the late imperial, Byzantine, barbarian and mature medieval periods, and with the history of medieval art. As will be remembered, the main centers of knowledge concerning the ancient world in the phases immediately following the universal triumph of Christianity are, apart from Rome itself, Ravenna, Constantinople, and many other places in both the East and West well known to archaeologists: e.g., Antioch, Ephesus, Hippo Regius, Arles, Tarragona, etc. But the deepest significance and fascination of Christian archaeology lie in the investigations directed at the very origins of the faith and the early days of its diffusion, and the search for evidence and confirmation of those historical events and persons, those beliefs, dogmatic definitions, moral aspirations, or ritual and liturgical traditions known to us from the New Testament and from apologetic and patristic writings, with all the emotive charge implicit in such a burning and delicate topic. It is easy to see why there is always such fierce argument around these studies and investigations. One is reminded, for example, of the endless discussions (not yet concluded) initiated quite recently by the presence of a sign in the form of a cross on the wall of a small room in Herculaneum. Interpretative judgment, too, is often affected by prejudices not connected with the critical value of the data, or functions with difficulty where sentimental propensities toward reverence, prudence, enthusiasm, or doubt are found.

Another area connected with the history of religion is the archaeology of Palestine — or, more generally, Oriental archaeology insofar as it touches on events, social backgrounds, or aspects of culture in any way connected with the Bible. For a number of years now

156. *View of the interior of the Christian Catacomb of Domitilla in Rome, with niches and arcosolium.*

there has been a very lively interest in these problems, which has not been confined to specialist scholars. It cannot be denied that at least some of the investigations and excavations in the East have been initiated, directly or indirectly, through the very appeal of themes from sacred history. Unfortunately the evaluation of their results has not always been entirely objective, through either excess of zeal or, on the contrary, preconceived skepticism. All the same, there exists today a vast and sound scientific knowledge of the topography and history of the Biblical lands, making possible the reconstruction of the background to events recorded in the Old and New Testaments. With regard to the historical nature of these events (and the cultural situation linked with them), archaeology has contributed substantially positive elements beyond the reach of prejudice. From such a serious and impartial modern scholar of Palestinian antiquities as W. F. Albright we can infer that present-day science is able to support tradition, even in the case of important and long-discussed

157. *Tomb near the grave of Clodius Hermes in the Catacomb of St. Sebastian in Rome, with stucco decoration. c.* A.D. *160.*

questions of testamentary criticism, such as the "Mosaic" antiquity of the Pentateuch and the date of the Gospels. An outstanding contribution has been made to our knowledge of Jewish religion and civilization at the time of the birth of Christianity by the discovery between the years 1947 and 1956, in caves and ruins near Khirbet Qumran, at the northern end of the Dead Sea, of manuscripts on leather rolls (and some on sheets of copper) — documents which seem to have belonged mainly to a community of members of the Essene sect.

From the nature and limits of the different archaeological activities so far described, the exceptional nature of the Vatican excavation mentioned earlier seems to stand out very clearly. This undertaking has in fact for the first time shown the supreme religious authority as the direct promoter of an investigation intended to solve, with the aid of modern archaeological methods, a historical problem of fundamental importance for the religious tradition of the Catholic

Church and for the very sources of its power: the question of the existence of the tomb of St. Peter the Apostle beneath the Byzantine and Renaissance basilica. Let us say at once that this work, carried out from 1939 to 1949 and then resumed in 1953 for further investigations (independently of the hope of sensational discoveries, which was encouraged by the legends that had accumulated for centuries around the historic site of the basilica, and in spite of disappointment and criticism), has led to results that are definitely favorable to tradition, as well as being remarkably important from the historico-cultural, artistic, and epigraphical points of view. In fact, a stretch of the ancient street of tombs has been found, probably the Via Cornelia, which ran alongside the Circus of Nero toward the slope of the Vatican Hill, along the longitudinal axis of the present basilica, with fine architectural tombs of the second and third centuries, adorned with mosaics, stuccowork, sarcophagi, and inscriptions. But there are also traces and indications of older depositions, of the first century A.D., particularly in an area which has been partially disturbed and rearranged, immediately below the High Altar. Here, in a spot corresponding with one of the graves and backing onto a wall painted red, is a little shrine with small columns, dating from as early as the second half of the second century — perhaps the "trophy of the Apostle" recorded in a contemporary source (Gaio in Eusebio, *Ecclesiastical History*, II, 25, 5 ff.). On the red wall, above a later transverse wall and in other places nearby, are numerous scratched inscriptions, difficult to decipher but certainly Christian and pre-Constantinian, which seem to allude to Peter; and in one of the sepulchral monuments of the necropolis, a short distance away, another such inscription, with figures, explicitly invokes the prayers of Peter for the good Christians "buried near his body."

One of the aspects of this excavation which has puzzled many scholars is the way it has been conducted — not so much technically as psychologically; and this has also aroused unjustified skepticism. There has been a certain amount of uncertainty and vagueness over the results, whereas one would have expected a clear statement and evaluation of them. The secrecy enveloping the work, especially at the beginning, the hesitation in divulging news of it, the premature or delayed announcements, the prevention of inspection by experts of other nations, and various matters which have remained persistently obscure, all indicate clearly that the emotional element in the approach to the work has not been overcome. (The investigation of such a sacred place may even have seemed to some to have been a violation of it.) When all is said and done, the apparent timidity displayed is an understandable reaction against the boldness of the program initially conceived and undertaken.

This episode of the excavation of the site of St. Peter's tomb is a particularly instructive one. It warns us of the dangers implicit in bringing scientific undertakings — in the present instance, archaeological ones — into conflict with the contradictory state of mind

158. *Column XXI of the seventh Dead Sea Scroll.*

191

which expects and accepts certain results from them but at the same time desires or fears these results. This attitude, much more widespread than one would think even in areas entirely outside the religious field, has up till now particularly characterized the problems of that department of archaeology still anachronistically called in some circles "sacred archaeology," as opposed to "profane archaeology" (meaning all the rest). But it should by now be unnecessary to point out that there is only one kind of archaeology, with its historical objectives, its methods, its techniques, the experience of individuals and of schools, its full and absolute scientific autonomy, whatever the fields of inquiry. This corresponds, moreover, to that respect for the freedom of genuine scientific research which is being

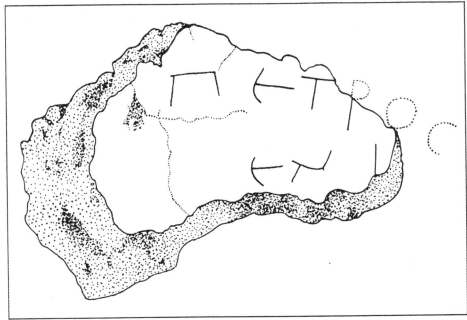

159-61. *Finds from the excavations of the tomb of St. Peter beneath the Vatican Basilica. Left, graffiti in the Tomb of Valerius in the Vatican necropolis. There is a sketch of the head of Christ and of St. Peter, and on it is scribbled a prayer to them: " Petrus roga per sanc(ti)s hom(ini)bus Chrestianis ad co(r)pus tuum sep(ultis)." This evidence predating the construction of the Basilica of Constantine confirms that this was the burial place of the apostle. The tomb itself has been located in a trench where the so-called Red Wall, with a tabernacle, was placed in the second century. Above, reconstruction of the tabernacle. Below, graffito on the Red Wall with the name of Peter.*

more and more happily confirmed in the thought and practice of the Church, even in connection with other problems touching closely upon archaeological studies — such as those concerning the origins of man, primitive civilizations, Biblical antiquities, and the like. In the last analysis this reflects, even on the religious plane, the conviction that there cannot exist two different truths which contradict one another.

## Beyond antiquity: the origins, development, and diffusion of human civilizations

Just what do we understand by "antique"? Apart from the current widespread significance of the term, a particular shade of meaning attaches to it whereby the concept "antiquity" acquires a relative sense with regard to our own period and civilization. A European would define antiquity without any hesitation as the classical civilization of Greece and Rome, submerged during the period of the barbarian invasions and revived during the Renaissance. European cultural supremacy may have given this idea, like so many others, the appearance of universal validity. But in fact, as soon as we move away even slightly from the center of the historical, humanistic Western traditions, the outlook is distinctly different. Without even leaving Europe, one can quote a curious example: Ireland, whose medieval and Christian civilization continued and developed without interruption, in language, traditions, institutions, customs, and art, the protohistoric Celtic civilization of the Iron Age. Ireland did not have an antiquity in the classical sense. (Indeed, the same could be said of the other Nordic European countries which remained outside the Roman Empire, but the case of Ireland is symptomatic because of the particular strength and nobility of her national traditions.) In Constantinople, on the other hand, antiquity lasted, after a fashion, without a break until the Turkish conquest in 1453; so that in the late Byzantine world, already seething with humanistic ferment, the survival and the rediscovery of antiquity are paradoxically united.

When one moves away from the Mediterranean and Europe, it is clear that the terms antiquity, Middle Ages, modern age, as applied, for example, to the cultural history of India or the Far Eastern countries, have only a chronological application. In America, ancient

194

and modern are divided by the European discovery and conquest. More generally, in the areas of ethnological culture in Africa, Oceania, and America — where in places prehistory itself continues to exist today — the term "ancient," or rather, "archaeological," to use the technical term employed by the ethnologists, is applied to all traces of life earlier than the nineteenth century.

Archaeology as the study of and search for ancient monuments originated, we need hardly repeat, in connection with the idea of antiquity possessed by the men of the Renaissance and of modern Europe, who were aspiring to rediscover a tradition and a historic patrimony of their own, one to which modern men could feel they were the legitimate heirs. This is valid for classical antiquity. But the idea

*163, 164. The influence of the classical world never touched Ireland, which passed directly from prehistoric to medieval culture. Left, stone with spiral decoration at the entrance to a late neolithic tomb at New Grange. Right, medieval bronze crucifix decorating a book cover. National Museum, Dublin. The style and decoration belong to the Celtic tradition.*

of archaeology directed to the study of their own origins and the revelation of their past glories also found favor, with the nineteenth-century growth of national ideologies, when applied to the particular area of culture of the individual European nations. It achieved fruitful results, and aroused much praiseworthy enthusiasm; but it must be admitted that it was also the cause of exaggerated emotions, sentimental and political, which have sometimes debased the objective sincerity of the studies. Such was the case with the overevaluation of Nordic prehistory by German scholars, or the excessive importance which has sometimes been attached to Celtism in France, or Romanism in Italy.

With the beginning of archaeological exploration in the Near East,

197

*165. Egypt during the Old Kingdom: statue of a scribe in painted stone from the necropolis at Saqqara. Fifth Dynasty, c. 2500 B.C. The Louvre, Paris.*

however, Europeans found themselves faced with the unforeseen. Over and above what the Greeks and Romans had known and inherited from those civilizations (and which for good or ill became part of the familiar picture of classical culture), extraordinary and unexpected new vistas were opened up, back into the depths of time. They revealed so many and such varied manifestations, such a wealth of historical experience, such great achievements of human thought, architectural and artistic creations of such impressive grandeur and quality, and so refined a way of life, that one is tempted to make a complete reversal of the traditional view of the antique world. Instead of seeing the history of the Eastern peoples simply as a preface to the great history of Greece and Rome, one is inclined to regard Greek and Roman history as the concluding chapter in an impressive story of a civilization which grew and flourished for thousands of years between western Asia and the Mediterranean. Egypt revealed its fantastic world of advanced organizational power, of magico-

COLORPLATE XVI. *Statue of Tutankhamon in the sanctuary of Karnak at
Thebes. Eighteenth Dynasty,* c. 1350 B.C.

166. *Ancient civilization in Mesopotamia: bronze head, probably of King Sargon I of Akkad, from Nineveh. c. 2350 B.C. Iraq Museum, Baghdad.*

167. *Egypt during the New Kingdom: King Akhenaten kissing his small daughter. Relief from Tell-el-Amarna, Eighteenth Dynasty, c. 1350 B.C. State Museums, Berlin.*

religious inventiveness and introspection (of which the Pyramids will always remain the indelible records), and of perfect formal abstraction as far back as the Old Kingdom of the third millennium B.C.; then the legislative wisdom, the sensitive moral profundity, the refinement of taste of more recent periods; the temples, the decorated tombs, the precious objects, the texts which preserve the records of the military undertakings and the building programs of the pharaohs of the Eighteenth and Nineteenth Dynasties, and the extraordinary attempt at religious and aesthetic reform made by King Akhenaten, who died about 1350 B.C.; the luxury surrounding the imperial court of Thebes (revealed in an amazing fashion forty years ago by the discovery of the treasure of Tutankhamon's tomb); the prestige of the priests and priestesses of the god Amon; finally, the solid continuity of a civilized tradition which, through all the varied changes of decadence and renaissance, innovation and reaction, expansion and foreign invasions (in later years by Lybians, Ethiopians, Assyr-

168. Seated lion. Iraq Museum, Baghdad.

ians, Persians, Greeks, and Romans), remained viable and retained its own unmistakable character for more than thirty centuries, from its prehistoric origins to the end of the ancient world.

More complex, but no less fascinating, has been the accretion of a picture of the civilizations of the Near East, the original center of all human progress, with its early farming cultures and the first works of architecture, the first cities, the first temples ever to be built, so far as we know. (Jericho in Palestine and Çatal Hüyük in Asia Minor, discovered recently, go back to at least the seventh millennium B.C.) We know about the painted pottery and the beginnings of metallurgy in Iran and Mesopotamia; the extraordinary intellectual and artistic flowering of the Sumerians of the fourth and third millen-

169. *Late civilization in Mesopotamia: reconstruction of the Ishtar Gate at Babylon, with revetments of enameled tiles decorated with bulls and fantastic animals. Seventh or sixth century* B.C. *State Museums, Berlin.*

170. *Persian civilization of the Achaemenid dynasty: rock-cut tomb of Darius III at Persepolis. c. 335-330* B.C.

niums (revealed by the famous discoveries of the tombs at Ur and elsewhere); the subsequent unfolding of the long history of the Semites of Mesopotamia (the civilizations of Babylon and Assyria), who were to impose their religious, literary, judicial, and artistic prestige on much of the East, and finally, in the first half of the first millennium B.C., their political power as well; the active and brilliant manifestations of life in the centers of Syria, Phoenicia, and Palestine, constantly open to the triple influences of the Asiatic hinterland, Egypt, and the Mediterranean lands; the civic development of the peoples of Asia Minor culminating in the Hittite empire of the second millennium, and inherited by the Syrio-Hittite states, the Phrygians, Lydians, Lycians, Carians, etc.; the marginal cultures

171. *Aspects of prehistoric civilization: rock art of the late paleolithic period. Figure of a mammoth in the Breuil Gallery of the grotto at Rouffignac, Périgord, France. It belongs to the Magdalenian period and can be dated between 15,000 and 12,000 B.C. Examples of fauna which became extinct during the late ice age are represented with astonishing realism. They were intended to insure successful hunting.*

of the Armenian and Iranian plateaus and the Caucasus, with the kingdom of Urartu, the Scythians, the Medes, etc.; and finally, the universal empire created by the Persian Achaemenid dynasty between the sixth and fourth centuries B.C., when all the previous experiences seemed to converge. Needless to say, this panorama of knowledge, so briefly indicated here, was revealed to human eyes in an order the reverse of chronological, beginning with the more recent civilizations (already well known a century ago, such as the Persians or Assyrians) and proceeding to the more remote ones, which are still in process of being discovered.

Oriental archaeology has revealed a type of antiquity which differs in form and proportions from that of the classical world. Without local continuity — because of the rift between past and present caused by Islam and the Ottoman empire — and only indirectly linked with the origins of Western civilization, the antiquity of the Near East presented an object of study entirely free from any ideological, nationalistic, or commemorative implications, a field of research where the main incentive was, on the contrary, curiosity for something new, the pure pursuit of knowledge. The work of those who pioneered exploration and excavation in the East thus marked, without their being aware of it, a decisive turning-point

COLORPLATE XVII. *Peruvian mask of the Chimú civilization. Collection Mujica Gallo, Lima.*

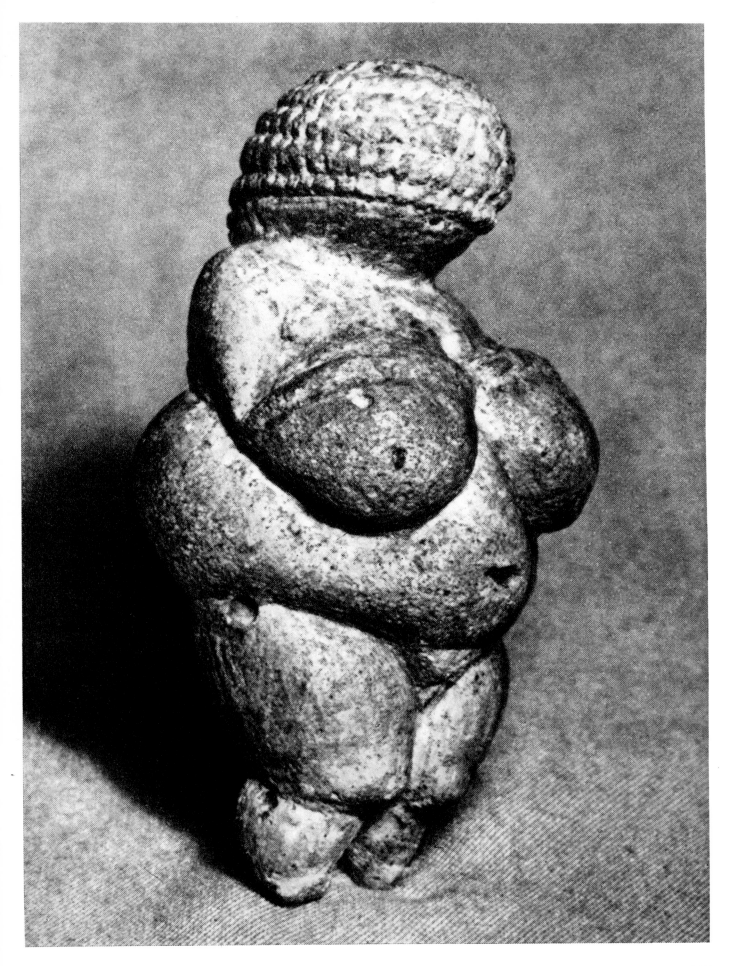

ON PAGE 207

172. *Late paleolithic art: the Venus of Willendorf. A plump, faceless female statuette of the Aurignacian period. c. 30,000-20,000* B.C. *Such figures were probably part of a fertility rite. Natural History Museum, Vienna.*

173. *Neolithic art: stylized female terra-cotta statuette from Strelice in Moravia. Third millennium* B.C. *Brno Museum, Czechoslovakia.*

in the history of archaeology, and a radical transformation of its concepts. The idea of seeking and rediscovering the foundations of a familiar world of their own was replaced by that of exploring and discovering for the first time worlds hitherto unknown. Thus they made the first daring leap beyond antiquity in the classical and Western meaning of the term.

Another advance of even greater magnitude was achieved through the progress made by the natural sciences. In about the middle of the nineteenth century, these were beginning to outline a geological history of the earth and its forms of life infinitely longer, more remote, and more complex than had hitherto been suspected on the basis of the current ingenuous traditional interpretation of Biblical data. Starting with the moment when Jacques Boucher de Perthes recognized near Abbeville in France the presence of man-made flint tools among the fossil remains of extinct animals on some sites of the geological Quaternary period (nowadays reckoned to be about 500,000 years ago), the study of primitive men and civilizations which we now call prehistory has advanced with increasing rapidity over the years, and has produced most impressive results, arousing the interest of countless investigators.

174. *Art of the bronze age: schematic human mask reversed onto a bronze sheet. From Mendolito near Adrano, Sicily. Seventh century* B.C. *Syracuse Museum, Sicily.*

Within the framework of changes in environment, and based on the evolution of man-made articles, prehistory was subdivided, as we know, into the following main periods: the paleolithic or old stone age (the period of chipped stone tools) corresponding to the Quaternary period, when there existed a human type different from modern man, and when the only means of supporting life was the hunting of wild animals; the mesolithic, which is essentially a continuation of paleolithic culture at the beginning of the present geological era (also known as epipaleolithic); the neolithic or new stone age (the period of polished stone tools), characterized archaeologically mainly by the diffusion of pottery (in fact some scholars, such as R. Pittioni, would like to call it the age of pottery), during which agriculture and husbandry originated, permanent settlements were established, and the first hints are found of the rise of the great early civilizations; the transition from the neolithic period to the age of metals, with phenomena which vary from place to place and are not always clearly classified — a period known as chalcolithic or aeneolithic (i. e., the age of stone and copper, or of stone and bronze); then the bronze age, and finally the iron age, corresponding to and contemporary with the growth of the great historical civili-

209

zations of the Near East and the Mediterranean. It must be realized that this classification, and the further division of the periods mentioned, originated in Europe and is applicable mainly to European prehistory. Elsewhere, different classifications apply — in large parts of Africa, for example, where the ethnological cultures of the present-day Negroes (a kind of iron age) are often superimposed directly on cultures of a paleolithic type. One must also correct the instinctive tendency to measure the various great periods of prehistory on the same chronological scale. In fact, one is dealing with a vast spiral of time which narrows down from the fantastic duration of the lower and middle paleolithic age (over half a million years) to the shorter but still considerable upper paleolithic and epipaleolithic periods (about thirty thousand years) and finally to the very brief neolithic age, the age of metals, and the historic period up to and including the present day (a mere few thousand years, with an ever-increasing rate of development).

Prehistory can be regarded in a sense as "pure archaeology";

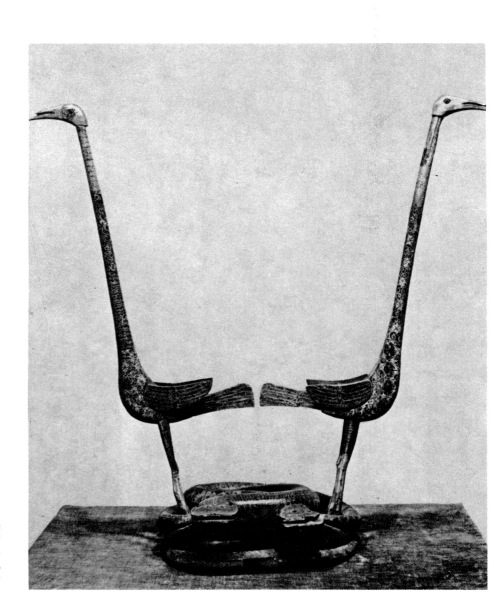

175. Aspects of civilization in Asia. Chinese art of the Chou period: a lacquered wooden gong support, cast in the shape of two cranes with serpents. Seventh to third centuries B.C. Cleveland Museum of Art. Wade Collection.

COLORPLATE XVIII. *Woolen cloak with embroidered figures from a tomb at Paracas, Peru. Museum für Völkerkunde, Munich.*

ON PAGE 213
*176. Detail of an Indo-Greek relief from Gandhara showing an ascetic praying before a Buddha. Third century* B.C. *Museum, Peshawar.*

*177. Above, aspects of Pre-Columbian art in America. Architecture in the Andes: view of the city-fortress of Machu Picchu in Peru, which flourished under the Inca Empire. Fifteenth century* A.D.

OPPOSITE

*178. Art of Central America: stucco head of a young man wearing a feather headdress. Classical period of Mayan civilization, fourth to tenth centuries* A.D. *From the Temple of the Inscriptions at Palenque. National Museum of Anthropology, Mexico City.*

while our knowledge of the historical civilizations of the ancient world also draws to a major extent on written traditions, prehistoric cultures are known — inevitably — only from the data of the surviving material remains. From these we obtain all the elements with which to attempt the reconstruction of man's painful progress, through a long struggle for existence, in the hard conditions of life in the great ice ages which followed one another in the Quaternary period; to delineate the successive types and races of mankind (whose fossilized skeletal remains are the province of paleoanthropology); to form an idea of the lives of these hunters, food gatherers, and primitive agriculturalists, in caves and in the open — their technical skills, their hopes, their superstitions. Among the different kinds of evidence found and assembled is some which speaks more directly to our imagination, arousing our admiration and our human sympathy: that in which primitive man expressed in figurative form his world and his talents — in other words, his art, particularly the rock

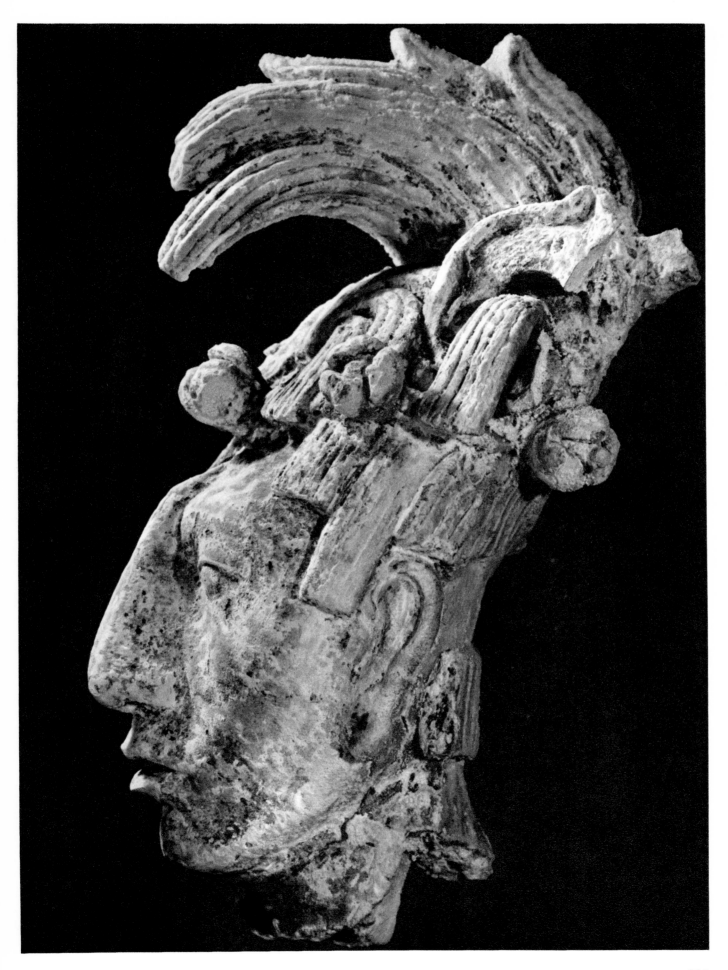

179, 180. *Two terra-cotta heads, from Jamaa (left) and Nok (right) in southern Zazia, Nigeria. Style of the Nok civilization, third to second centuries* B.C. *Jos Museum, Nigeria.*

paintings and engravings of animal subjects, so incredibly realistic, going back to the upper paleolithic and epipaleolithic periods. In all its fields of study, however, prehistoric archaeology, by necessity implicit in its very nature, has led to a refinement in methods of investigation, to the precise placing of finds in their natural surroundings, to the observation of every detail, which was lacking in traditional archaeology and which represents a fundamental element of progress in the technique of excavations.

"Beyond antiquity" means, finally, the universal extension of archaeological inquiry, along the co-ordinates of space and time, to the whole of humanity's past, on every continent. During recent decades we have seen the birth of the archaeology of Africa, India, Central Asia, China, Japan, Oceania, and America. It has been particularly successful in the lands with the greatest wealth of ancient monuments, such as the Indian subcontinent (where, for example, the discovery of the Indus Valley civilization, of Harappa and Mohenjo-daro, reunites us with the protohistorical world of Iran and Mesopotamia in the third and second millenniums B.C.), Central Asia (with the fascinating revelations of the civilizations of the Altai, the Caucasus, Khwarezm, etc.), the Far East (where the historical civilizations of China and Japan seem to have been introduced by an

*181, 182. Aspects of Eurasian civilization. Above, gold model of a chariot from the Oxus Treasure, seventh to sixth centuries B.C. British Museum. Below, gold group of a lion tearing a horse to pieces. Scythian art. The Hermitage, Leningrad.*

217

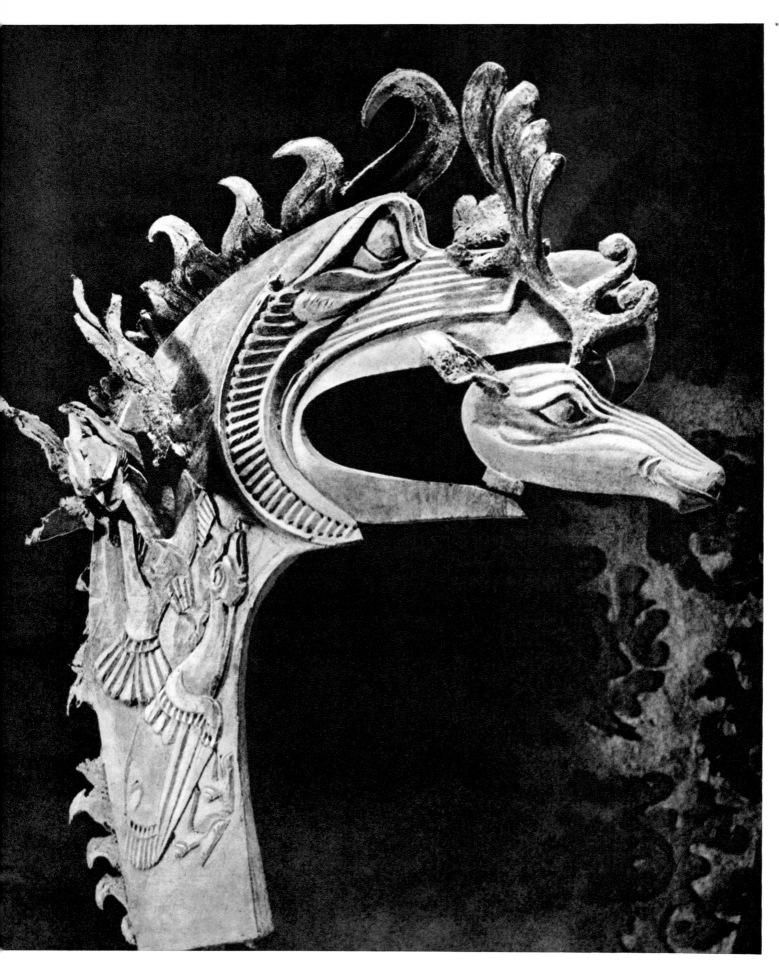

OPPOSITE

*183. Animal art of the steppes: wooden ornament with leather decoration depicting a head of a griffin biting a stag. From one of the princely tombs of Pazyryk in the Altai, fourth or third century* B.C. *The Hermitage, Leningrad.*

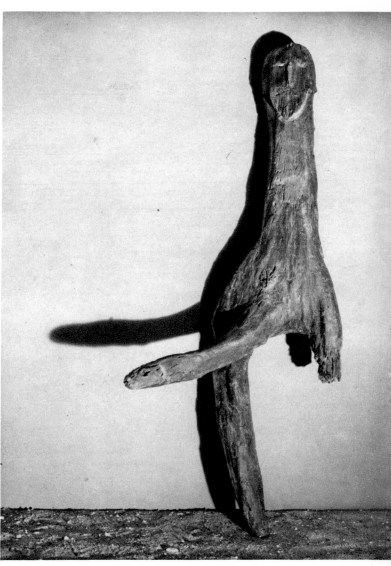

*184, 185. Left, classically inspired Celtic silver coin showing stylized head. First century* B.C. *Cabinet des Médailles, Paris. Right, phallic wooden figure of the Scandinavian god of fertility. From a bog at Broddenbjerg near Viborg in northern Jutland. Late bronze age or early iron age, fifth or fourth century* B.C.

imposing series of prehistoric cultural phases not unconnected with the West), and finally, the territories of the great Pre-Columbian civilizations of Mexico, Central America (Guatemala, Honduras), and South America (Peru, Bolivia, and Colombia). More and more clearly, indeed, we see the arresting work of archaeology reaping rich rewards in the reconstruction of the origins, the varying rate of development, and the interrelationship of human civilizations. One can already faintly perceive the possibility of deep-seated connections linking the greatest and most ancient centers of human progress — those of western Asia and the Mediterranean and those of eastern Asia and America. Little by little we are even finding out more about the remote building-up of European experience, through perceiving the influence exercised on this continent in the neolithic period and the age of metals by the Near Eastern civilizations, and the more fluctuating and spasmodic but no less active influences from the Asiatic steppes, joined later by the direct action of the classical world on the barbaric Hallstatt and La Tène periods. (In this connection, the recent discovery of a princely tomb of the late sixth century B.C.,

186-90. *Aspects of barbaric and early medieval art and civilization. Above, a lion keeping watch. National Museum, Stockholm. Center, the Midgard Serpent, detail from a Viking woodcarving, ninth to eleventh centuries* A.D. *Bottom left, golden flask decorated with a horse and rider in relief. From the Treasure of Nagyszentmiklos, Rumania, eighth to ninth centuries. Kunsthistorisches Museum, Vienna. Bottom right, wooden head found in the lake region near Jankau, Poland, from early Piast times. Poznan Museum. Opposite, a wooden cart with carved ornamentation, from a Viking burial trove found beneath the Oegsburg ship. Ninth century. Museum of Viking Ships, Oslo.*

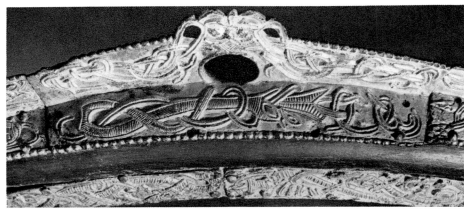

220

at Vix near Châtillon-sur-Seine in France, containing objects of gold and bronze, is very telling, as are the explorations at Heuneburg in Germany.) Eurasian protohistory also has links with the whole world of the "barbarian" cultures of the migration period from the end of antiquity and the beginning of the Middle Ages. This has now become a positive and fruitful region of archaeological research, carried out mainly by German, Scandinavian, Polish, and Russian scholars. This breath-taking opening-up of horizons seems to characterize the new aspect of present-day archaeology, and has almost changed the meaning of the word. Once, "archaeologist" meant one who studied marble copies of statues by Polyclitus or Praxiteles in museums. Nowadays, it usually means the excavator of neolithic strata at sites in Asia Minor or Palestine, the Mayan temples in Mexico, or the medieval dwellings at Novgorod in Russia. But this does not mean that the traditional themes of archaeology have been superseded, particularly as regards classical art and civilization, as is proved by the enduring vitality of these studies in Europe and America. It has simply become clear that they have taken their place as part of an infinitely vaster world of problems and learning.

191, 192. *Aspects of medieval archaeological finds. Above, the excavations of the foundations of a round church with two apses, from the ninth century, discovered near Hodonin, Czechoslovakia. Center, the excavated foundations of a ninth-century church with a sepulchral chapel and a baptistery. Uherskè Hradiste, Czechoslovakia.*

193. *The ruins of the fortifications at Bydgoszcz, Poland. Lusatian culture, 550-400* B.C.

# ARCHAEOLOGY IN ACTION:

## THE SEARCH FOR ANTIQUITIES, THEIR CONSERVATION

## AND INTERPRETATION

### The men concerned: the fortunes and methods
### of archaeological discoveries

Even today, the idea of archaeology still conjures up in the minds of a great many people the image of the lucky discoverer of buried objects. What we have said so far, however, goes to show that the achievements of archaeological research go far beyond the simple dig, and far beyond the initiative and ability of single individuals. They cover every possible form of reconnaissance and study of ancient remains, and are brought to completion in the historical interpretation of the discoveries — requiring, among other things, a tradition, a wide range of experience, and adequate means.

Some discussion is therefore necessary of archaeological activities from the practical point of view, considering their different aspects and interrelationships from the aspect of the single basic objective — the increase of our historical knowledge. Ideally, we can visualize this work as a sort of great cycle of operations, comprising the professional training of archaeologists, the selection of instruments, the planning and organizing of the work, the topographical sizing-up and analysis of the site and the monumental remains, the actual excavations with all the concomitant observations, the gathering-up, conservation, possible restoration, and classifying of the remains and objects discovered; finally, the scientific evaluation and the publication of the discoveries (including the more general work of classification, comparison, and synthesis on historical, cultural, and artistic problems, based on various archaeological sources and finds). All these activities form an essential part of the sphere of interest of archaeology and archaeologists, and concern all kinds of problems and fields of study — not only purely scientific matters (the historical disciplines, geography, anthropology, etc.) but also teaching, the use of techniques, the protection of monuments, restoration, museums, publishing. This plurality of functions affects the archaeologist's choice of a field, and his work. In addition, it renders indispensable the co-operation of other skills outside archaeology, and in general involves a vast network of collaboration in the world of culture, administration, production, etc.

Of course, in discussing archaeology in action one must first know the protagonists — the archaeologists themselves. No one, I am sure, will question the essential importance of the human factor in the absorbing and delicate operation of evoking ancient human civilizations through the study of their surviving fragments. For all that one may visualize an archaeology based on the accurate working of a collective labor machine, or transformed into an exact science of calculation and measurement by apparatus, it is clear that the laying-down of lines of inquiry, the singling-out of problems, the manner of observing details, the interpretive reasoning and intuition, will always depend on the character, the perception, and the scholarship of individual observers. In this respect, the progress made by archaeology substantially reflects the increasingly mature outlook of archaeologists. The growth of these studies, or their stagnation, results (as in all other scientific and cultural activities) from emergence of vigorous minds or from the prevalence of mediocrity, at any particular time or place. Of particular importance is the selection of the men, their education, the creation of scientific schools and traditions of the highest standard and unassailable prestige, characterized by unflagging zeal, so as to guarantee for archaeological research a constant flow of trained and intelligent specialists. It can and must be stated, therefore, without hesitation, that the teaching of archaeology is always complementary to, and inseparably associated with, the actual practice of archaeology.

In the history of archaeological discoveries, the human factor is revealed, brisk and self-confident, with all its qualities and capabilities, even its eccentricities; with its instinctive perception, subtlety of deduction, and tenacity of purpose. And with it is combined another element, external and imponderable — the element of luck. In reality, archaeological research, with its driving enthusiasm and the margin of uncertainty which determines its outcome, closely resembles a hunt, or, as we said at the beginning, a police investigation. Its success can depend, according to circumstances, on the skill or flair of the investigators, a well-organized plan, or a stroke of fortune.

As we know, some of the famous discoveries have come about in an entirely fortuitous and unpredictable manner. Apart from earlier instances, there is the episode, already mentioned, of the Rosetta Stone. The Venus de Milo, which was to become as celebrated as other famous classical statues like the Laocoön and the Apollo Belvedere, was picked up in pieces on that island by a Greek peasant in 1820. The treasure of Ziwiyeh, with its splendid gold, silver, and ivory articles of Scythian and Assyrian workmanship, came to light by chance in 1947 in a locality not far from the city of Sakkiz, in Iranian Azer-

194. The Venus de Milo was discovered in 1820 by a peasant on the island of Melos in the Cyclades, brought to Paris, and placed in the Louvre. The statue dates from the Hellenistic period and was soon famous as one of the masterpieces of antique sculpture.

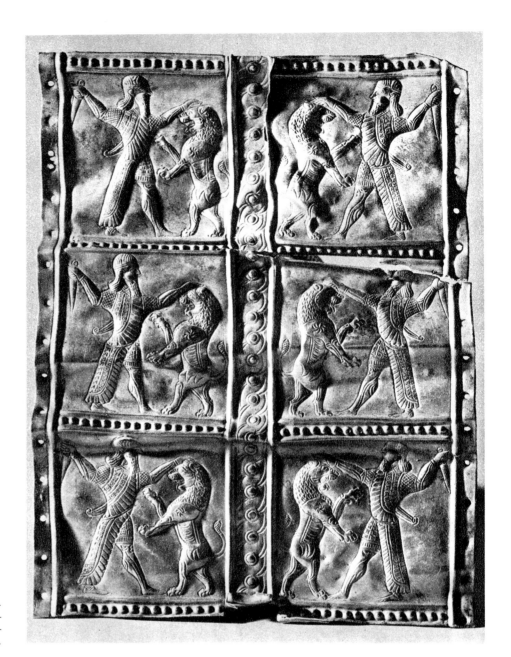

195. *Gold plaque decorated in the Assyrian style, from the treasure discovered in 1947 at Ziwiyeh, Iran. Seventh century* B.C. *Museum, Teheran.*

baijan (and it might be added that many of the strange proto-Iranian bronzes from the region of Luristan, now sought and studied with so much interest, are the result of casual and unsupervised discoveries by the local population). In the same year, 1947, an event occurred in the East which had all the fascination of an Arabian Nights story. The Bedouin shepherd Mahommed ed-Di'b, wandering among the rocks on the shores of the Dead Sea in search of a stray goat, penetrated into a cave and saw a row of earthenware jars. Believing them to be connected with sorcery and the *djinn*, he fled in terror to fetch a companion. They returned together and opened the jars in search of treasure, but found only scraps and fragments of skins. These, coming into the hands of more knowledgeable merchants, proved to be the first pieces of the famous Hebrew and Aramaic scrolls of Khirbet Qumran. But the most celebrated case of all — the classic example, as it were — is the event to which we owe the revelation

228

196. One of the huge bison paintings in the cave of Altamira in Spain. The paintings were discovered quite by chance by a child in 1879. The revelation led to the discovery of the prehistoric rock art of the paleolithic period. The Altamira polychrome figures, which are drawn with forceful naturalism, mark the climax of this art in the Magdalenian period.

of the whole of prehistoric cave art. This occurred in 1879, and its protagonist was a twelve-year-old girl. Visiting a cave during a country excursion, her youthful eyes alert for anything odd or strange, she observed the outlines of some enormous figures of animals, and urgently drew the attention of her father, the scholarly Marcelino de Sautuola, to them. Her exclamation, "Papa, mira los toros pintados!" has become a byword in the history of archaeology, as a cry of wonder at the sometimes incredible surprises of chance (of which there are certainly more to come).

However, we should not exaggerate the importance of chance and luck. It is often alleged (with a certain amount of malice) that archaeologists always arrive late on the scene of the major discoveries, and their more laborious researches only succeed in producing scraps. But if one remembers the revolutionary value of some of the revelations, and the incalculable riches brought to light as a result

G. BELZONI.

197, 198. Left, G. B. Belzoni (1778-1823), who was one of the first to explore Egypt and her monuments. From a lithograph by C. Hullmandel. Right, H. Schliemann (1822-1890), who discovered Mycenae and Troy.

of calculated undertakings, it is easy to see that this is a mistaken impression. One has only to consider Schliemann's excavations at Troy and Mycenae, those of Ludwig Borchardt at Tell-el-Amarna (the city of the reforming Egyptian pharaoh Akhenaten), Sir Leonard Woolley's exploration of the fabulous Sumerian tombs at Ur, and the discovery of the sanctuary of Hera at the mouth of the Sele in Campania by Paola Zancani Montuoro and U. Zanotti-Bianco (an example of investigations worked out and planned at the desk, following indications in ancient texts), to realize that such criticisms are not consistent with the facts. Moreover, even the great chance discoveries could never have had any scientific or cultural significance had their importance not been recognized, had they not been admired, discussed, placed in proper archaeological and historical context and integrated with subsequent investigations and discoveries. The sight little Maria de Sautuola beheld would have had no future history if her father had not undertaken to interpret it, publicize it, and defend its importance resolutely in the face of scholarly skepticism.

*199, 200. Left, Sir Arthur Evans (1851-1941), who through his excavation of the Palace of Knossos in Crete discovered the Minoan civilization. From a painting by W. Richmond, 1907. Right, U. Zanotti-Bianco (1889-1963), leader of archaeological research in southern Italy, standing among the excavations of the Temple of Hera at Foce del Sele.*

The biographies of archaeologists present a varied, almost kaleidoscopic assortment of origins, inclinations, predilections, characters, and achievements. The story of their adventures sometimes reads like a novel, and in any case is full of moving and exciting episodes. We come across dedicated men from all walks of life, drawn by circumstances into the circle of archaeology and held there by the beacon of vocation — not as a hobby (as it would now be called), but as something that wholly absorbs their minds and energies. The Englishman Layard, the first great excavator of the Assyrian monuments, was such a man. So, too, was Boucher de Perthes, the excise clerk who discovered the Quaternary period of mankind, and Schliemann, who, before devoting himself for many years to the disinterring of buried worlds, had been a merchant, exporter, and banker. Another character of the same kind was the American traveler and diplomat J. L. Stephens, to whom we owe the exploration of the monuments of the ancient civilization of Mexico. As archaeological research became more and more rigorously scientific, professional archaeologists took the lead, most of them coming from the ranks of historical scholars (classicists, Orientalists, ethnologists, etc.), though quite a number of those devoted to prehistory are naturalists who have been attracted to archaeology. Some of these scholars also seem to have inherited the adventurous spirit and the insatiable enthusiasm of their predecessors in the Romantic era. It is precisely out of this combination of a sound training with an inquiring mind, farsightedness, and tenacity that there emerge the great militant figures of the world of archaeology, to whom we owe the major discoveries of the last hundred years. Among these are such famous names as G. Dörpfeld, T. Wiegand, R. Koldewey, W. M. Flinders Petrie, G. de Mortillet, P. Orsi, Sir Arthur Evans, Sir Leonard Woolley, A. Maiuri, H. T. Bossert, and Sir Mortimer Wheeler. Men of different temperament, as we have already illustrated in connection with the history of classical art, showed a preference for the considered study of archaeological monuments and objects, their classification and interpretation, and historical criticism in general — not only in the field of classical studies, but also in those of Orientalism and prehistory. (In the latter connection, one cannot omit V. Gordon Child.) It is therefore understandable that in the cycle of archaeological activities described above, some scholars choose (it may be at different points in their career) one rather than another of the practical functions inherent in the common discipline. These include, apart from direct research on the site, scientific organization, direction of museums and institutes, university teaching; and administrative or teaching duties at their own center often alternate with digging expeditions abroad — especially in the case of archaeologists from areas not particularly rich in antiquities of their own, such as Northern Europe and the United States.

The obtaining of genuine scientific results from discoveries and the progress of archaeological studies depend fundamentally on good methods of investigation. This implies a sound historical grounding (with, of course, emphasis on various specialized points) and adequate technical experience in topography, the conduct of excavations, the classification of the structures and materials of ancient artifacts, etc. It also requires, as an absolute essential, a capacity for strict inductive reasoning, based on the principle that nothing can be stated without proof, and that even the so-called working hypothesis must be based on concrete indications. However, soundness of method in the work of modern archaeological science is reinforced on a practical level by direct co-operation among scholars, and even among research and study organizations — in the responsible public departments, scientific institutions, universities, foundations, expeditions, and associations. The individual capacities of the archaeologists tend nowadays more and more to be integrated and turned to account in co-operative undertakings. At this point, attention must be drawn to the great importance of "collaborators," whether they be young specialist assistants and students (archaeologists in embryo, so to speak),

COLORPLATE XIX. *The steps leading to the upper floor of the east wing of the Palace of Knossos.*

the old type of assistant or overseer of moderate learning (gradually disappearing even in Italy, though in past years their flair has played a most useful part in that country), technical coadjutors such as architects, draftsmen, photographers, restorers, etc., or the actual specialist manual workers, sometimes incredibly expert as regards sites and excavating, and no less enthusiastic than the archaeologists themselves. From outside, valuable contributions are made by those engaged in the natural sciences — biologists, chemists, and physicists. Finally, I would like to add to this list all those cultivated members of other professions who pursue archaeological studies as a personal interest, and collaborate with scholars and the authorities in pointing out and salvaging ancient remains, and who sometimes carry out their own modest investigations, especially in the field of prehistory. Within its limitations, this partnership is also of great value. But a whole range of marginal activities remains inimical to the interests of science and the archaeological inheritance: those of the amateurs without method, adventurers, clandestine excavators, and dealers in antiquities who swarm around the places richest in ancient remains, whom we have already discussed elsewhere.

## The tools: modern techniques in the service of archaeology

We often have the feeling that, in opposition to a traditional humanistic archaeology, essentially the work of men, there is also a supposed modern technical archaeology, based on apparatus. This polemic derives its origin from the rapid and intense growth during recent decades — one might even say in the last few years — of the application of sciences like chemistry and physics to analysis of soils and ancient artifacts, in the carrying-out of research, and the interpretation of archaeological data, particularly in Great Britain, Scandinavia, the United States, and Italy. One wonders if — and how far — the archaeologist with the old type of literary and historical education will be replaced by the scientist or the technician, who is already able to discover and map out buried monuments by means of aerial photography or electromagnetic instruments, or to assign definite historical dates to any ancient objects containing carbon. But the question is really an idle one, because the methods of investigation as such always remain a means to an end — historical interpretation — and because the interpreter of the discoveries, whatever his education (even if it is technical and scientific rather than historical and literary), will not be able to carry out his task efficiently and conclusively if he does not do it in his capacity as, and with the mental attitude of, an archaeologist and historian. At the most, we can recognize that some archaeologists are more receptive than others to the new contributions made by scientific techniques, and more convinced of their results. There are also scientists who, in their enthusiasm for the application of the methods of physics and chemistry to the fascinating field of archaeology, claim to have solved all its

201. *Modern techniques of exploration. Aerial photograph showing the outline of a neolithic village near Foggia in Apulia. Note the lines of the double enclosure around the circular inhabited area, with the huts, which are themselves circular, within it.*

problems already. But this is quite understandable in view of all the changes and advances taking place today in the type of equipment used in archaeological research.

In fact, the whole history of archaeology is characterized by the willing acceptance of new means of investigation — even, at times, the search for them. They can be recognized in the help given by the other sciences in supplying data, methods of application, or even general criteria of orientation, particularly in the case of the naturalistic disciplines of geology, anthropology, ecology, and paleontology, whose convergence on the sphere of archaeology, especially prehistory, brought about a fundamental change of direction in the second half of the nineteenth century. Practically the whole conception of environmental and stratigraphical excavation, all the laboratory analyses (of marbles, metals, woods, etc.), much of the sociological, technological, and economic observations concerning ancient civilizations, are the direct result of the collaboration between the natural sciences and archaeology. But it should also be pointed out that archaeologists did not hesitate to adopt for their own ends all the

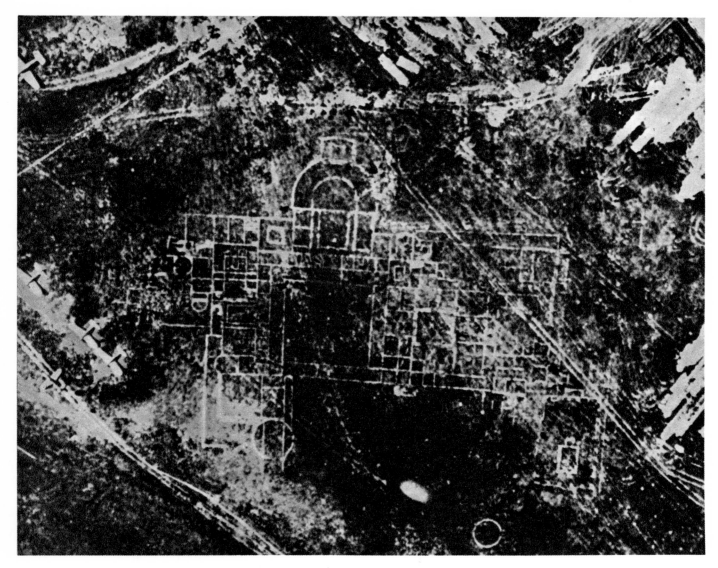

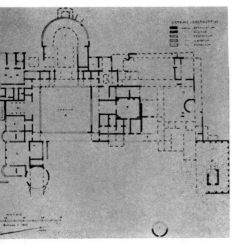

202, 203. Aerial photograph and ground plan of a large Roman villa of the Imperial period beneath the Centocelle airfield near Rome. The plan of the villa can be clearly seen in all its details.

inventions and technical aids as they became available. In this connection I would like to mention once again the fundamental part played by photography, as a means of reproduction and documentation, in the development of modern scientific archaeology.

At the present time, this progress seems to have reached a culminating point, even an explosive one. Assistance is supplied by information from the most varied scientific fields, and equally varied types of apparatus, some of it specially devised for archaeological research — and this is the most important innovation. Furthermore, its application extends throughout the whole cycle of archaeological operations and activity: from the aerial, surface, and subterranean reconnaissance of the ground to the methods of conducting the excavation; from the analysis of materials and objects to the processes of dating, conservation, and restoration. We can therefore divide scientific techniques as applied to archaeology into four main sectors: (1) techniques of exploration; (2) techniques of analysis; (3) techniques of dating; (4) techniques of conservation and restoration.

The first of these concerns the procedures for the identification

204. *Aerial photograph of the ancient city of Paestum in southern Italy. In the center the area of the Greek temples and other religious and public buildings already excavated can be clearly seen. Beyond is the network of streets with their rectangular pattern. Aerial photography is especially valuable in the study of ancient town planning.*

of ancient remains and for facilitating their excavation. In the past, topographical reconnaissance — other than that based on data from ancient sources and learned and local traditions, on information collected in various ways, and on the guidance of ordinary maps or plans — depended exclusively on the exploration of a territory on foot, with patience and with keen eyes, by cultivated explorers or by scholars. One remembers, for example, the English archaeologist T. Ashby, who in the early decades of this century explored the neighborhood of Rome and the consular roads of Italy, collecting a great number of observations now for the most part irreplaceable. The traditional archaeological maps were compiled by this method. If it was desired to undertake excavations in a particular area, the work was almost always carried out by taking as a starting-point a ruin visible above the surface, or some other external sign — the presence of fragments of ancient pottery in the ground, stones artificially shaped, trees and bushes grouped in a certain way, which had a special significance for the old excavators. Or the presence of hollow chambers could be detected by tapping on the rocks. In the necropolis of Spina, where the old Etruscan tombs are buried in the mud below the water level of the lagoon, the official archaeolo-

205. *Aerial photograph of Ostia Antica, Italy.*

gists, as well as clandestine ones, have made use of a long iron rod to "feel" for the objects and ascertain their position. Dowsers also carried out investigations, trying in particular to find objects made of metal — an embryo forerunner of modern electromagnetic experiments.

Today we have completely new methods available which make it possible to obtain exact and reliable information over large areas, and with the maximum saving of time and energy. For the purpose of topographical prospecting, archaeology has at its disposal an incalculably valuable and almost miraculous means of reconnaissance — that of aerial photography, enabling an area to be recorded photographically from above. The application of this procedure to the discovery of ancient remains, which dates back to the years between 1930 and 1940, was considerably increased by the photographic records made on the mosaic system by Allied air forces over enemy-occupied territory during the last war, and was perfected and brought into general use in the succeeding years, particularly through the efforts of the Englishman John Bradford. Air photographs, whether taken perpendicular to the ground (vertical) or at an oblique angle, reveal things invisible to an observer on the ground: for example,

239

the coloration, or the intensity of light and dark areas, which varies according to the humidity, the density and nature of the vegetation, the presence or absence of debris in the ground; and, when the light is at a low angle, the shadows cast by irregularities in the ground indicate the existence of hollows and trenches, of leveled or paved strips (streets), of ramparts (embankments, earthworks), and the walls of buildings beneath the level of the soil. This process operates mainly in a synthetic capacity, isolating the traces of ancient works from the natural features of the site. Among its most important early achievements are the discoveries of numerous prehistoric and protohistoric dwellings in England and Italy; the radiography of the Etruscan cemeteries of Cerveteri and Tarquinii; the delineation of the Roman frontier fortifications (the *limes*) in North Africa. Nowadays, however, the system is in use throughout the world, and forms the indispensable basis for preparing all precise archaeological maps and plans.

An additional method of archaeological prospecting, which can be used to determine the area and extent of ancient inhabited sites, is chemical analysis of the soil, carried out by taking samples over a large area and measuring the percentage of organic elements, especially phosphoric anhydride. Through this process the density and duration of human occupation can be calculated. This already takes us, however, into the realm of techniques for the direct observation of the ground and subsoil, applied principally at a practical level to facilitate investigations within limited areas by indicating the whereabouts and extent of walls or cavities (such as subterranean tombs cut out of the rock), and for measuring the depth of archaeological stratification. In this connection we might mention the seismic method, which records the various effects of reflection or refraction of the shock waves caused by an explosion through ground of varied nature and texture. At present, however, great progress is being made, particularly in Britain, in the study and application of geophysical methods based on measurement of the electrical resistivity of the ground, and on variations of the electromagnetic fields depending on the quantity of solid bodies present. (These last, recorded by special instruments, including the proton magnetometer recently brought into use with great success, can also transmit signals indicating their nature — for example, the presence of metal.) In addition, certain mechanical devices are being tried out, particularly in Italy, such as the Nistri periscope — a kind of probe equipped for the observation and photography of subterranean areas not yet excavated. It is well known that with these instruments, in combination with other prospecting techniques, the Lerici Foundation of the Milan Polytechnic has carried out extensive exploration in the Etruscan cemeteries, and as a result has discovered a number of new painted tombs at Tarquinii. (As many of these tombs were found in a five-year span recently as had been found in the previous century and a half.)

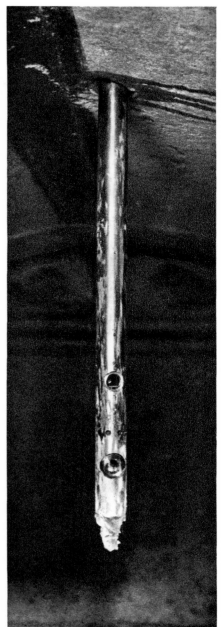

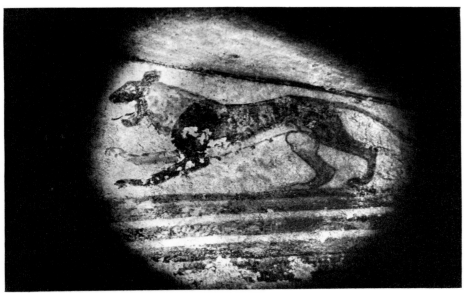

206-8. Equipment for subsoil archaeological research belonging to the Lerici Foundation at the Milan Polytechnic. Above, periscopic sounding rod at work outside and inside an Etruscan tomb. Below, detail of a wall painting in a tomb at Tarquinii which has not yet been opened. This photograph was obtained by the periscopic rod.

These remarkable inventions have a particular application in countries where the traces of early civilizations are few and far between, scattered over vast areas, as in the northern districts of Europe, Asia, America, or other regions of limited historical development, whereas they seem unnecessary (at least in the same way and for the same purpose) in the Mediterranean lands, which abound in ancient monuments well known both historically and topographically and still in process of investigation. Thus the use of the methods of geophysical prospecting for the direct purpose of discovering ancient settlements and for the organizing of excavations must always be commensurate with their ability to produce results, according to the circumstances, the requirements, and the limits of the scientific control necessary in archaeological investigations, apart from the conservation of monuments. Furthermore, it would be a mistake to regard them simply as a means of extending the work and speeding it up, though they are certainly capable of this, owing to their enormous technical potentialities; for the principle of maximum output is obviously in opposition to the character and aims of the projects of study of which these methods are the tools.

Techniques of analysis are applied to the study of rocks and stones used in ancient buildings and sculpture (especially marble, hard stones, etc.), metals and their alloys, terra cottas, glass, organic materials used for practical or decorative purposes, such as ivory and bone, wood, amber, and fibers. In this kind of investigation, the natural sciences also come to the aid of archaeology in any matter involving the classification of vegetable remains (plants, seeds, fruit, etc.), the remains of food and drink, bones of animals, or even human skeletons. This analytical aspect is generally justified by providing a more thorough and intimate knowledge and description of archaeological objects. Scholars concentrating on artistic or typological problems often find this irrelevant or too difficult; and, indeed, what does it matter whether a carved gem is carnelian or sardonyx, or whether an ax or a sword was cast in one kind of bronze alloy rather than another? In fact, however, the very thoroughness of these investigations brings out more and more clearly the exact significance of certain details — the provenance of a particular quality of marble, for example, or the presence or quantity of copper, zinc, lead, or silver in a particular alloy — in establishing the locality of works of art, trade currents and routes, the dating of objects, and the identification of the culture to which they belong — in other words, for the acquisition of essential historical and cultural information. At the present time, the main countries concerned with prehistoric and archaeological studies have numerous laboratories for petrographical analysis, physical analysis (particularly for the study of metals by means of spectrography), and chemical analysis, operating principally or exclusively in the service of archaeology. Among those concerned with metals are the laboratories and working teams at Nancy, Oxford, Stuttgart, and Baku. But it must be pointed out that this field of investigation is still in its infancy, and at the empirical and tentative testing stage, compared to what it may ultimately contribute in the future to our knowledge of ancient civilizations.

There is, however, one branch of analytical science which during the last few years has grown at an enormous, almost a giddy rate, and which must be considered in a separate category because of the unique character of its objective. This is the form of analysis directed to establishing, in absolute terms, the age of materials and objects. The so-called dating techniques represent a sensational development, inasmuch as they oust all previous attempts at chronological reckoning based on the traditional historical eras (for example, the dates of Roman history calculated *ab Urbe condita*, those of the Olympiads for Greek history, the computations derived from what is known as the Sothic cycle for the history of Ancient Egypt, etc.), or on lists of kings and dynasties, adding up the numbers of years in each reign (Egypt, Mesopotamia, etc.), and, where documents are lacking, the presence of more or less datable objects (as with the Cretan and Mycenaean civilizations in relation to that of the Orient), or even on an approximate estimate of the depth of deposits corresponding to specific phases of protohistoric or prehistoric cultures. It is easy to see that these criteria are subject to the uncertainties and errors of the ancient historical sources, and to a high degree of subjectivity in our reconstructions. Modern science, however, promises to make it possible for ancient remains to divulge their age directly, by means of the physical and chemical study of the material of which they are composed. At the moment, we are dealing with what is mainly a theoretical possibility, and it can be claimed that the various procedures described are still in the experimental stage. But they already hold out rich promise of very encouraging results. Among the methods of dating, some also include the calculation of the geological periods preceding or contemporaneous with the appearance of man, purely in the field of natural history. We shall confine ourselves here to those uses which concern archaeology.

It has been known for a long time that the age of trees can be deduced from the growth rings of the trunk, usually corresponding to a similar number of annual growing seasons. But the width and characteristics of these rings vary according to the warmth and rainfall of the season which produced them. As this is relatively uniform for all the individual plants, it is possible in principle to determine correlations based on a scale of variants forming a kind of absolute universal calendar, capable of dating, within limits, woods of unknown age. This is the method of "arboreal rings," or dendrochronology. Another type of "natural calendar" was suggested by the Swedish scholar G. de Geer: the examination of the deposits left by the annual thawing of the glaciers, or *varve*, relatively constant in different places. By analyzing the plant pollen contained therein and synchronizing the study of the deposits with the variations in the limits of glaciation, a vast and reliable series of successive climatic

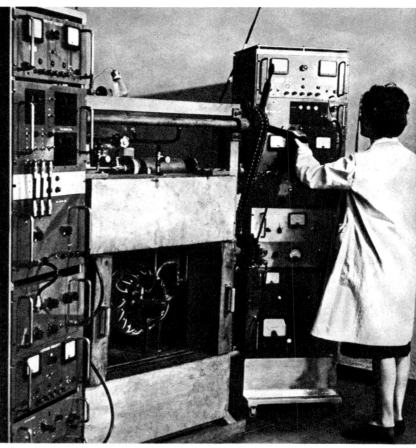

209, 210. Modern research techniques. Left, use of the proton magnetometer to detect hidden walls and cavities. Right, apparatus belonging to the Nuclear Geology Laboratory at Pisa University for measuring the age of organic remains by the Carbon 14 method.

cycles has been reconstructed continuing to the last great expansion of the ice, particularly in Scandinavia; and the succeeding human civilizations from the end of the paleolithic age to the beginning of historical times have been related to it, with definite dates. This method is also known by the name of geochronology. There are other systems applicable to particular classes of remains, such as the measurement of the fluorine content of bones, either animal or human, or the analysis of the iron materials found in earthenware, whose properties are definitively fixed at the time of firing, and correspond to the terrestrial magnetic field (known from other sources) at that particular moment.

But by far the most important and most promising dating technique, whose fame is beginning to reach even the general public, is the so-called radiocarbon method, invented in the United States in 1946 by the atomic physicist W. F. Libby. This is based on the principle that every living substance contains and conserves a constant amount of Carbon 14, a radioactive isotope of the normal Carbon 12, fed by cosmic radiation. With the death of the organism, there immediately begins the disintegration of isotope 14, and the radioactivity of the carbon is uniformly reduced by half in a cycle of about 5,700 years. In theory, the measurement of the proportion of radiocarbon found in any buried organic substance (wood, peat, the shells of shellfish, bone, etc.) enables its age to be established automatically; that is, the moment when a tree was cut down for its wood, or

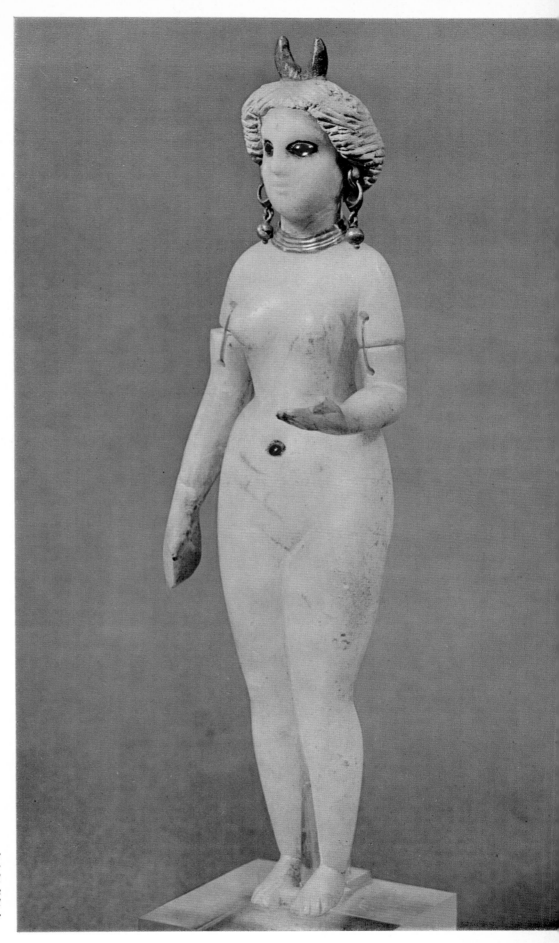

COLORPLATE XX. *Hellenistic statuette of a female divinity from Babylon. The body is made of alabaster, the eyes and navel of rubies and gold. This is a typical example of the use of several materials in a work of art. The Louvre, Paris.*

when a shellfish was eaten. It therefore tells us the age of a particular archaeological complex. In practice, the calculation is complicated by the extreme delicacy of the measuring process, which requires involved and costly apparatus, perfectly adjusted and sheltered from outside radiation, and samples completely free from contamination with more recent organic substances. The measurement is really made up of a series of data grouped between an upper and lower limit, and the older the sample the greater the degree of oscillation. Moreover, the intrinsic minuteness of the initial quantity of Carbon 14 has hitherto limited the efficacy of the measurement to no more than some ten thousand years. There is also the possibility, for the moment incalculable but pointed out with increasing insistence by those who look on this method with reserve and skepticism, that variations in the intensity of the bombardment with cosmic rays in the past, and considerable increases in atmospheric radioactivity at the present time, may have an adverse effect on the accuracy of the calculations. In spite of this, the radiocarbon method, supplemented by repeated and consistent measurements and above all by checking against other sources of dating, including historical ones, has already made it possible to construct a coherent chronological framework which goes back from the historical period to the neolithic cultures (about 7000 B.C. for the Near East), the Mediterranean and European epipaleolithic (about 10,000 B.C.), and the upper paleolithic (roughly from 40,000 to 10,000 B.C., in round figures); and similar classifications have been made for North American prehistory. Clearly, if history in the traditional sense is mainly built up on a succession of dates, we have to recognize that with the new dating techniques we are rapidly approaching an amazing, hitherto unimagined, positive integration of prehistory with history.

Finally, modern science, techniques, and production are constantly providing new discoveries to aid the work of salvaging and protecting ancient wall structures of soft stone, unbaked brick, etc., or bronzes threatened with oxidation, other metals, and above all the perishable organic materials of ancient furnishings — for example, wood (especially when found under water or in damp conditions), bone, basketry, textiles, and the like. But all this belongs, properly speaking, to the sphere of restoration, and to a large extent falls within the orbit of applied craftsmanship.

ON PAGE 248

*211, 212. Important monuments of the past preserved for millenniums. Above, the pyramids of Cheops, Chephren, and Mycerinus rising out of the desert plateau at Giza. They are still among the most gigantic creations of man. First half of the third millennium B.C. Below, remains of the ziggurat of Nanna at Ur, Mesopotamia, 2250-2050 B.C.*

### Reconnaissance and excavation

Every large-scale excavation in a particular territory, or undertaken with the intention of bringing to light some particular aspect of the ancient world, is preceded by a period of preliminary exploration of the territory itself and a study and investigation of its monuments.

COLORPLATE XXI. *Temple of Queen Hatshepsut at Deir el Bahari. c. 1480* B.C.

213. *Temple-observatory called El Caracól at Chichén Itzá, Yucatán, Mexico. Architecture of the Maya-Toltec period, between the eleventh and fourteenth centuries* A.D.

This has always been the case, beginning with Rome in the classical world (i. e., Italy, Greece, the Hellenistic East, and then Egypt, the Near East, India, Central America, etc.), and it is still true of more narrowly limited archaeological areas and problems. Sudden discoveries due directly to excavation without any previous indications are extremely rare, and depend on special circumstances. The famous examples are Pompeii and Herculaneum, where the superimposed volcanic deposits (lava, ashes, and lapilli at Pompeii, solidified mud at Herculaneum) had almost completely covered and hidden the ancient remains. In a different way, the discovery of the Mycenaean and Cretan civilization was linked with the personal and literary incentive of Schliemann's exploit, with a reinterpretation from a new historico-archaeological viewpoint of the surviving monuments of that period already known in antiquity, such as the walls of Mycenae itself, and of Tiryns. As a rule, therefore, the uncovering process begins with a chance discovery which arouses curiosity and attracts attention to the area. It proceeds with the reconnaissance of the ruins visible above ground level and the collection of local antiquities, and it culminates in the actual excavation.

Nevertheless, the topographico- archaeological study of a particular region or a particular place, the marking out of the monuments, the classifying and publication of the sculpture, epigraphy, and other ancient objects existing on the spot or recovered in various ways, should not be regarded simply as a prelude to excavation, as a kind of

214-17. *Ancient monuments still standing. Below, polygonal walls of Cori, near Rome. Fifth or fourth century* B.C. *Right top, stone circle at Stonehenge, Wiltshire, an important megalithic sanctuary. First half of the second millennium* B.C. *Center, the Parthenon, Athens, 447-432* B.C. *Interior view. Bottom, Temple of Bacchus at Baalbek, Syria. Interior of the cella. Second century* A.D.

218. *Western portico in the Forum of Trajan, Rome, which looks onto Trajan's Market. Having survived amidst later buildings which have been dismantled, the Market has now been fully excavated and restored.*

subordinate activity, preparatory and incomplete. In fact, the vast majority of the archaeological evidence we now possess comes not from beneath the ground (or, at least, not from an actual exploration below ground level), but has been found on the surface. It comprises (1) works or buildings which have been preserved throughout the centuries (sometimes abandoned and reduced to ruins, more often at the hands of man than by nature), as exemplified by the Greek temples at Paestum — the most impressive and magnificent intact complex of its kind in existence; (2) those protected by the abandonment of the unhealthy coastal scrubland; (3) the monuments which have survived in the deserts of Africa and Syria and the jungles of southern Asia and Yucatán — often preserved intact, or restored, or kept in continuous use (like the Pantheon in Rome). There are also

253

219. *Aerial photograph of the center of Naples, showing the intersecting street plan which is part of the original Greek design. Many towns in Europe still maintain their ancient street network and are thus living monuments of antiquity.*

254

256

statues and other works of art which have been handed down from antiquity to our own day, together with gems, precious vases, and goldsmiths' work from religious and secular treasuries. And finally, there are fragments which have been incorporated into more recent buildings, and various kinds of antiquities which have been known from time immemorial and which formed part of the earliest archaeological and art collections. We may also add that certain living aspects of the ancient world's tangible creations still survive, which, independently of the total or partial survival of the original fabric, are preserved in the town plans of historic cities such as Naples, Turin, Cologne, or Vienna, where the placing of some of the ancient streets and town gates has remained unchanged.

The importance of archaeology which has been handed down (in comparison with that which has been excavated) may surprise a great many cultivated persons who are not specialists, and who regard excavation as a magic word. But it is a fact that the study of the road network of Italy or the Roman Empire; the identification of the regular divisions of the level cultivated ground, according to the Roman system known as *centuriatio*; the comparative history of the

*220, 221. Ancient monuments still standing. Above, Roman bridge at Rimini. Early first century* A.D. *Below, Imperial Roman aqueduct at Maintenon-sur-Eure, France.*

*222. Ancient monuments still in use. The interior of the huge tepidarium of the Baths of Diocletian in Rome was converted into the Church of Santa Maria degli Angeli by Michelangelo, with additions by L. Vanvitelli.*

223. *Ancient works of art preserved above ground. Huge head of a divinity in the funeral sanctuary of King Antiochus of Commagene (69-31 B.C.) at Nemrut Dag in southern Anatolia.*

growth of cities with a regular chessboard plan in Greece, Italy, and the East — a field of study now very highly developed, particularly with the help of aerial photography — are among the most fascinating problems of modern archaeology, and are almost unconnected with the work of excavation. The same can be said of the whole task of diligent exploration, critical observation, architectural drawing or graphic reproduction, interpretation, study, and publication in connection with great monumental complexes or individual monuments, from the painted and engraved caves and rocks of prehistory to the Egyptian temples, from Roman buildings to Christian basilicas, from the Indian *stupas* or the paintings in the Ajanta caves to the sacred buildings and sculpture of Mexico. In these cases, too, there was no archaeological excavation, no essential period of digging before the ancient monument could be brought to light. If there was any digging at all, it assumed a subordinate and subsidiary role, completing our knowledge of the monuments, cleaning up their foundations,

COLORPLATE XXII. *Air view of the nuraghic village at Barumini in Sardinia. First half of the first millennium* B.C. *Before excavations were carried out, only isolated nuraghi were visible. Now the fortress can be seen on the left, towering above the densely built circular huts of the village.*

224. *An ancient work of art handed down to posterity. Cameo with busts of the Emperor Honorius and the Empress Mary, dated* A.D. *398. During the Middle Ages it was kept in Constantinople and set in a filigree gold frame. It is now in the possession of the Rothschild family in Paris.*

checking on the chronology and technique of the initial stages of their construction and growth, and eventually becoming a preparation for strengthening and restoring them — to no greater extent, be it noted, than happens in the study and restoration of medieval and modern buildings.

On the other hand, topographical reconnaissance and the location of monuments can, as we already know, develop into a more thorough and radical investigation of ancient sites, involving the uncovering and salvaging of their buried remains — in other words, precisely what we call, in the archaeological sense, excavation. The connection between ancient monuments visible on the surface and the idea and objective of excavating is an accepted thing (though an excavation can also be undertaken on the basis of historical traditions, news of earlier finds, faint surface indications, and, nowadays, photographic prospecting from the air). Sometimes, known monuments represent the surviving nucleus of an imposing hidden reality, much

261

225, 226. Excavations of entire monuments in the East. Above, detail of the brickwork beside the west door of the citadel at Harappa, Pakistan. Third millennium B.C. Below, view of the sanctuary of Amon at Karnak, Egypt. It contains buildings from the Twelfth Dynasty until the Hellenistic period, although the majority belong to the period of the great pharaohs of the Eighteenth and Nineteenth Dynasties (c. 1580-1200 B.C.). In the right foreground, the sacred lake; in the distance, the obelisks of Hatshepsut and Tuthmosis III; in the center, the Great Hall of Ramesses II; to the left, the west and south columns of the Hall.

as the peaks of a submerged continent rise like islands from the sea; and when these emerge from their isolation they may take on unexpected significance. For example, the great pyramids of Giza, celebrated for thousands of years for their abstract architectural qualities, have acquired a concrete historico-religious background through the discovery of the funerary temples built at their base. In another field, the famous nuraghi or dolmens of Sardinia, generally regarded as isolated fortresses of the ancient inhabitants of the island, have now been shown by excavation to be military and religious edifices that stood like an acropolis above considerable centers of habitation. Sometimes the visible monument may itself be formed by the progressive accumulation, over hundreds and even thousands of years, of the rubbish and deposits left by human activity and building within a confined area, creating an artificial hill — typical of the plains of

*227, 228. Above, view of the palaces of the Achaemenid kings at Persepolis, late sixth to early fourth centuries B.C. In the foreground, the Room of the Hundred Columns; a little behind, the Audience Chamber of Darius and Xerxes. Below, the sanctuary of Apollo at Delphi; descending from the upper level, note the theater, the temple of Apollo, the monuments of the Sacred Way, and, in the background, the rocks known as the Shining Ones.*

the Near East with their very ancient and highly developed civilization, and known by the Arabic word *tell* (or the Turkish words *tepe* or *hüyük*).

As must by now be abundantly clear, archaeological excavations are a means of acquiring knowledge, and not a hunt for antique objects. There is a fundamental difference in attitude and in aims, particularly as regards our present-day activities. It must be admitted that even the uncontrolled and destructive excavations of the past, carried out for the sole purpose of removing statues, paintings, mosaics, vases, and other remains, with complete disregard for their original setting and accompanying circumstances, were also understood as a search for knowledge. In fact, the actual articles recovered (and made known) were themselves new pieces of evidence of ancient art and civilization. But modern archaeology has, as we know,

*229. The Processional Way at Babylon, with the Ishtar Gate in the foreground. First period of Nebuchadnezzar II (604-592 B.C.).*

taught excavators little by little that the value of a find lies chiefly in its relation to the monument, its position, the level at which it occurred, and (in the case of buildings, stores, tombs, etc.) the material found along with it. This awareness has become more acute outside the field of the major civilizations and the great monumental complexes, especially in regard to the more modest evidence of the ancient way of life, and particularly where prehistory is concerned — in other words, where the vast majority of objects have not the slightest value apart from that which they derive from belonging to a particular set of data. Now it is clear that once this awareness has been acquired, excavation as a means of learning demands a whole series of conditions, precautions, and increasingly accurate checking, not previously associated with such investigations. When an excavation is carried out with the sole intention of finding objects for pleasure or profit, it always aims at the acquisition of the maximum

230. The Etruscan sanctuary at Veii. The Apollo and fragments of other painted terra-cotta statues were once used to decorate the roof of the temple (sixth century B.C.). They are seen here as they appeared when they were discovered in 1916.

number of articles with the greatest possible speed. This is what happened in the past, and still often happens today. Now, however, we can see that such criteria contrast strongly, even dramatically, with the scientific method of excavation, insofar as they neglect or disperse any evidence concerning the conditions under which the find was made.

But even a properly organized excavation, carried out with the intention of obtaining new information, may exhibit defects of method, and a greater or lesser degree of care and efficiency. Because of this, one can divide archaeologists (professional archaeologists, that is) into those who know how to excavate and those who don't. Of course, there are all sorts of side issues which can have an adverse effect on the perfect carrying-out of an excavation, which are outside its strictly scientific ends. Some of these are considerations of personal or national prestige, the desire for spectacular results, the attitude

231-34. *Above, excavations at the palace at Phaistos, Crete, showing a cache of pottery vessels. Middle Minoan period, c. 1800-1600* B.C. *Below, a view of the excavations of an Etruscan sanctuary at Pyrgi, sixth to fifth centuries* B.C. *Opposite above, the Grotta dei Cordari in a stone quarry in Syracuse, dating from before the time of Dionysius the Tyrant. Below, excavations of the ancient wooden and stone fortifications of Poznan, Poland. Tenth century* A.D.

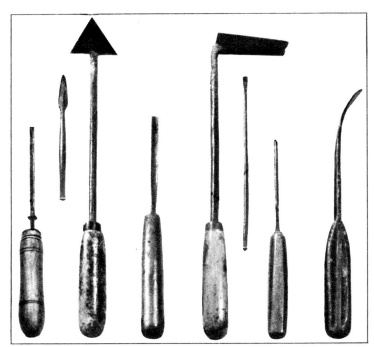

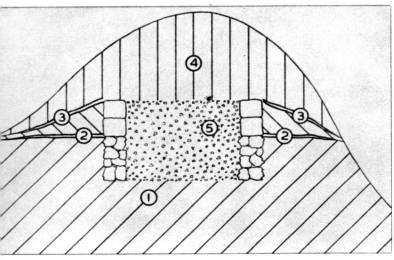

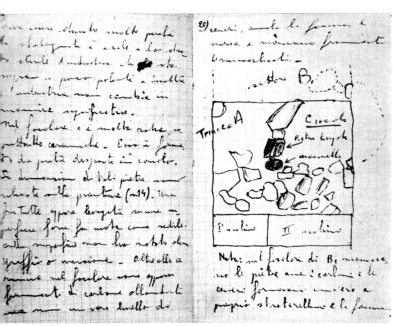

235-38. Above left, an example of paleolithic excavation carried out by the Instituto Arqueológico del Ayuntamiento de Madrid, in 1959. Center, section showing excavation at the Fortress of Johor Lama (Malaysia). It was built about 1547, destroyed in 1564, reoccupied, and finally destroyed by the Portuguese in 1787. (1) Subsoil; (2) layer of ash from the destruction of 1564; (3) layer of ash from the destruction of 1787; (4) rampart; (5) stone wall supporting the rampart. Excavation work was begun under Dr. W. G. Solheim in 1960. Below, an archaeological diary with descriptive notes and sketches. Above right, some of the instruments used in the excavation of prehistoric sites. Their use in conjunction with modern technical methods varies according to the site and its geological make-up.

COLORPLATE XXIII. *Archaeologists being trained under Professor André Leroi-Gourhan at the late paleolithic site (Chastelperronian) of the Grotte du Renne near Arcy-sur-Eure. The white and blue flags indicate the position of flints and bones which will be left* in situ *until the site has been completely explored.*

toward certain polemical questions. But in general the differences are more often connected with the constant progress and improvement in research methods which involve divergence of opinion, of outlook, and of technical training among archaeologists themselves. Thus the "new school" is in opposition to the "old school," a strictly technical approach conflicts with a traditional one, some minds being more superficial and others more receptive to the possibilities inherent in different situations and circumstances.

As already noted, the conducting of a modern excavation imposes a number of conditions and expedients which are now, on the whole, universally accepted as essential if the investigation is to attain its scientific objectives. In the first place, there must be adequate planning, implying at least a general idea of the historical problem connected with the excavation, and requiring a knowledge of the area and a preliminary investigation, with precise information on all previous discoveries and investigations, together with the preparation of general and specialized topographical maps, including cadastral charts (large-scale survey plans) where available. These are still better if integrated with good small-scale vertical aerial photographs, with a maximum ratio of 1:1000. Part of the program is to estimate how long the work will take, and whether it is likely to develop into several research campaigns, according to the ends in view and the financial means available. And then, of course, it must be organized. There are differences between short excavations limited by chance necessity, such as modern construction work, road building, intensive land reclamation and cultivation (the so-called *Notgrabung*, which in many countries, including Italy, is mainly under the supervision of the responsible State archaeological departments); major tasks of systematic archaeological investigation of sites and monumental complexes, supported by a permanent organization of local services (in Italy, this applies to Pompeii and Herculaneum, Cerveteri, etc.); and foreign or mixed expeditions, such as the French excavations at Delos, the American excavations at Sardis in Lydia, and many other similar instances. But in every case it is necessary nowadays for an archaeological excavation to be under the sole direction of a person of adequate experience, and constantly followed up throughout the site by professional archaeologists or at least by archaeological trainees. Assistants or nonspecialists must never be allowed to act in a supervisory capacity. There should also be available architects and draftsmen, photographers (a function which can be assumed by the archaeologists themselves), restorers, and possibly also specialist technicians for the investigation of the subsoil, geologists and paleontologists (for prehistoric researches), epigraphers (particularly for certain branches of Oriental archaeology), etc. If an excavation is to be properly conducted, whatever the particular situation, certain elementary rules must be observed. There should be a constant checking of all the material that emerges, the co-ordinates of surface and depth being noted: the first by laying a preliminary grid,

239-41. *Stratigraphical excavations. Torrimpietra, near Rome: above, section of the excavation with a series of Quaternary prehistoric deposits corresponding to the Riss glacial period (between 240,000 and 150,000 years ago); center, strata with archaeological traces of human activity alternate with volcanic materials and river and lake formations. In the lowest levels stone tools of Acheulean type have been found, and in the upper strata tools of Mousterian type. Below, archaeological stratification, facing the sea, of the Etrusco-Roman town of Pyrgi, with sections of a stone wall and rough bricks from buildings.*

the second in relation to the stratification of the subsoil. Observations are recorded descriptively in diaries or minutes of the excavation, and on them plans and sectional diagrams are based. The actual procedure adopted will depend on the circumstances and the immediate object of the operation. Preliminary investigations or trials may be carried out by cutting ditches or trenches; by digging up earth or sand deposits; by actual excavation of strata of specific archaeological interest. Then there are the complementary tasks of protecting the ancient constructions or arranging for their partial removal (where this is absolutely necessary for more thorough investigation), and provisional or permanent preservation of sections of the site for further investigation and inspection. Finally, there is all the work of organizing and clearing up the excavated area, and of putting in order, classifying, cleaning, administering protective "first aid," and restoring the material recovered.

Basically, the way in which modern archaeological excavation differs from the kind of investigation carried out in the past — and which in a way links the actual excavation with its critical interpretation — is the so-called stratigraphical method, so much discussed in recent years, and generally considered, rightly or wrongly, to be in the absolute sense *the* method of scientific excavation. This is based on the observation that the residues left by human habitation accumulate progressively, epoch by epoch, forming regular layers of artificial soil which may be deeper or shallower corresponding to longer or shorter periods of habitation (from the few yards' increase in depth of the soil of Rome or Athens between the classical period and our own day, to the vast accumulation of archaeological deposits in certain caves inhabited from the remotest prehistoric times). By identifying these strata and allocating them to known cultural periods it becomes possible to recognize precisely the cultural phenomena which have succeeded one another in each site, together with their relative chronology, inasmuch as the more recent cultures appear near the surface and the earlier ones in progressively deeper layers. In addition, a comparison between different stratigraphies makes it possible to establish the relation in time of their respective levels, and also to observe the cultural variations between one place and another at contemporaneous levels. The stratigraphical method is essential in archaeological investigations dealing with small traces distributed over a long period of time, as in prehistory — where, indeed, it originated. It is also generally applied now as a guide in the excavation of cities, buildings, and sanctuaries of more recent date. Nevertheless, it clearly has its limitations and drawbacks. The depth of the layers is not automatically equivalent to proportional lengths of time; the layers themselves are frequently not horizontal, but follow the contours of the ground beneath, sloping, indented, or in a parabolic curve (making very careful observation necessary in order to follow its true course); in addition, breaks, disturbances, and insertions occur. The value of this guide, therefore, must always

242-44. Underwater archaeological discoveries and research. Above, objects from the cargo of an ancient Roman ship wrecked off Mahdia in Tunisia, now in the Albenga Museum. Below, the salvaging of one of Caligula's ships in Lake Nemi, south of Rome, achieved by the partial draining of the lake. The hulls of the ships were subsequently destroyed by fire during World War II.

COLORPLATE XXIV. *Underwater archaeology. A Roman wine amphora discovered off the island of Giglio.*

245-47. Above left, equipment from the ship Daino belonging to the Centro Sperimentale di Archeologia Sottomarina, Albenga. We see it here at work on the sea bed searching for wreckage (see pls. 242, 243). Right, pieces of pottery with remains of the packing straw, found off the island of Giannutri in Tuscany. Below, broadside of one of the ships found in Lake Nemi (see pl. 244).

be checked, where possible, against other observations and by the historical data. For example, it is obvious that the presence of a neolithic flint tool in a higher layer than one containing a coin of Augustus does not mean that the neolithic is later than Augustus, but simply that the stratification has been disturbed. Moreover, there is no point in applying the stratigraphical method to certain types of excavation, such as the digging up of large buildings buried in the sand, exploring the interiors of tombs, etc. This may help to counteract the exaggerated importance allotted to it by some scholars and the fanaticism of amateurs.

Finally, we must also mention another kind of archaeological exploration which seems very fashionable today — submarine archaeology, or underwater excavation, as it is sometimes called. It will be remembered that in the past the sea has given up some celebrated finds, such as the splendid treasure of Hellenistic bronzes, marble sculpture, architectural fragments, terra cotta, etc., discovered in 1907 off Mahdia on the eastern coast of Tunisia, and preserved in the Bardo Museum in Tunis, or the colossal bronze statue of Zeus, or perhaps Poseidon, of the fifth century B.C., fished up off Cape Artemisium in the Aegean between 1926 and 1928. These are the cargoes of sunken ships. A notable example of the systematic recovery of underwater antiquities is the recovery, after many failures or abortive attempts (beginning with a project of Leon Battista Alberti), of Caligula's two famous ships — or, rather, floating pavilions — from Lake Nemi, near Rome, with their ornaments, structural details, and technical equipment, providing a considerable amount of information concerning the naval architecture of the Romans. This was made possible by draining away some of the lake and lowering its level. Unfortunately, the hulls of the ships were destroyed by fire during World War II. With the recent increase in popularity of underwater fishing, the search for and discovery of ancient remains under the sea has become so widespread that it has attracted the attention of scholars and of the authorities. Submarine archaeology, from being of only marginal interest, has become an important activity. In connection with the diligent study of ships' cargoes like those identified off Marseilles and off Albenga in Liguria, specialized scientific centers, started by F. Benoit and N. Lamboglia, have been established in Provence and Liguria. Specially equipped ships like the *Calypso*, the *Elie-Monnier*, the *Daino*, underwater photographic apparatus, diving gear, and dredging and salvage equipment have been made available for actual exploration. Meanwhile, interest has extended to include the whole Mediterranean (recently, for instance, the cargo of a ship of the Mycenaean period has been salvaged near Cape Gelidonya in southern Asia Minor), the Atlantic, and other seas. A sensational event of our own time belonging to this class of activity, though outside the range of archaeology, was the raising, between 1959 and 1961, of the Swedish warship *Vasa*, which sank off Stockholm in 1628.

### The conservation of antiquities: protection, restoration, museums

The English word "salvage" is nowadays understood to mean any action directed to the safeguarding of monuments of the past, particularly archaeological remains, from destruction. But there is implicit in the term itself a very real feeling of intense alarm for the infinite perils threatening this patrimony of mankind, and an urgent summons to a crusade in their defense. In fact, in recent years the problem has been on the agenda of international cultural organizations, and has been of active concern to UNESCO. Meetings like the symposium organized at the end of 1960 by the American Association for the Advancement of Science, and events of world-wide notoriety such as the inevitable submersion of the archaeological sites of Nubia as a result of the construction of the new Aswan Dam, have also brought the subject into prominence. This chance notoriety, however, and the general interest in the idea of salvage, should

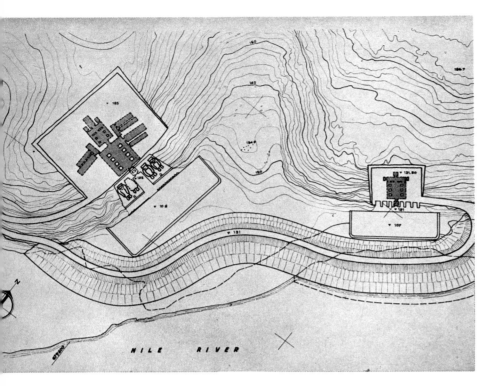

*250-56. Pietro Gazzola's proposals to save the temple of Ramesses II at Abu Simbel, in Upper Nubia. Left, plan of the two temples, indicating the parts to be rescued from the waters of the Nile. Below, diagrams of the steps to be taken to raise the larger temple.*

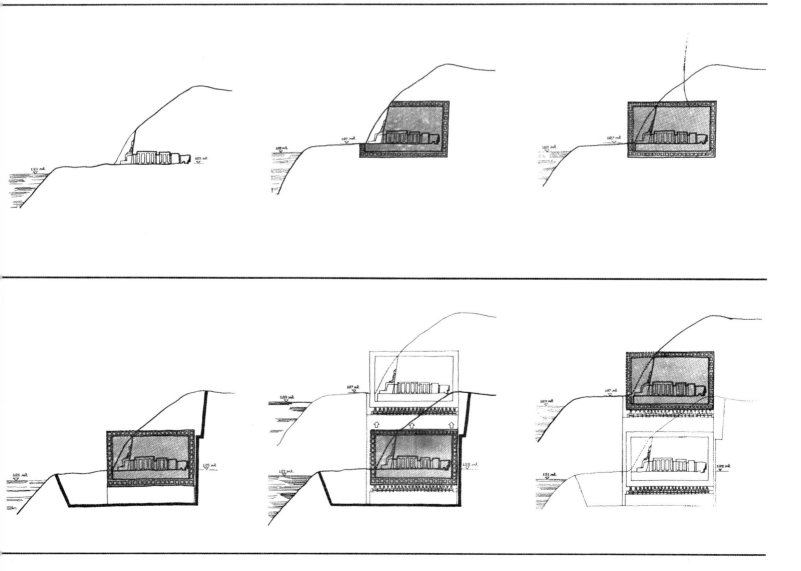

COLORPLATE XXV. *Rescue work on the rock temple of Ramesses II at Abu Simbel. The monument was moved piece by piece to a higher level. Here, the head of one of the colossi is being raised.*

not make us forget the enormous amount of traditional work carried out day by day, silently and patiently, by scholars and specialized institutions in every country, to protect from damage as far as possible the excavations as a whole and the material they provide, to save from more or less rapid decay the objects recovered, to strengthen ancient structures, to safeguard the monumental complexes, and to arrange the layout of archaeological sites and the material and works of art preserved in museums in a definitive, orderly, and at the same time clear and pleasing fashion.

It might be thought that this activity does not really further the scientific aims of archaeology — the increase of our historical knowledge — but belongs more to the province of culture, forming part of the intellectual and moral requirements of contemporary society. But it is not easy to separate the two, even theoretically. Concern with conservation has increased as the tasks of archaeological research have become more obviously an essential part of historical research. Since the information furnished by archaeology comes from tangible objects, there can be no doubt that the possession of evidence is identical with the possession of the object itself, and that the loss of the object is equivalent to the loss (or to a substantial depreciation in value) of the evidence. In fact, the observation and judgment of the discoverer does not exhaust the documentary possibilities of a find in the case of the remains of buildings, or groups of objects, or single ancient artifacts. The interpretation of these can be completed, or very much expanded, and sometimes actually reversed, by subsequent analysis, by later finds, and by the general increase of knowledge and progress of studies. We know all too well nowadays how little use, for critical purposes, is the information from destroyed monuments or lost works of art, however accurately they have been described, even when there are excellent reproductions. This applies to every kind of archaeological relic, but is particularly true in the case of figurative works: the original is irreplaceable. Within limits, on the other hand, the completion or restoration of an ancient monument or object, whether carried out on the object itself or in drawings, also contributes to an understanding of its significance. And, finally, the orderly display of archaeological finds in museums, quite apart from its value as culture or publicity, is intended for the particular advantage and assistance of scholars, functioning in much the same way as a library. It forms, moreover, the logical complement to the work of protecting and conserving antiquities. In fact, museums are often linked with institutes for archaeological research, with bodies responsible for the protection of monuments, and with laboratories concerned with restoration and analysis.

As we have already shown, the work of conservation begins with the actual excavation (where this is properly conducted, of course) if not even earlier. For example, no intelligent archaeologist would start digging out the base of a decaying wall without first strengthening or supporting it. But, as Sir Mortimer Wheeler rightly observes, all excavation, even at its best, is destruction. The inevitable losses caused by the removal of strata or of objects, or the disturbance of structures, must be weighed up shrewdly and swiftly by the excavator against the actual gain in data and the need for more thorough investigation. Besides, it is clear that the acquiring of information and the recovery of objects is a direct result of insuring the material safety of the maximum number of discoveries even under the most difficult conditions — discoveries which include not only the general configuration of the archaeological site, the ancient installations and the structures, but also the most infinitesimal traces of life and products in archaeological strata, sometimes (according to climate and circumstances) doomed to rapid and even immediate decay.

*257, 258. Nineteenth-century restorations. Right, the Arch of Titus in Rome before restoration, after an aquatint by D. Hawell. Opposite, the arch as it looks today, unencumbered. The missing parts were replaced with travertine by L. Valadier in 1821.*

284

Fragile or broken objects, or groups of objects linked together, can be removed by means of supporting frameworks or "beds," or the use of a strengthening agent (for example, paraffin wax). The work of recovering wooden relics from the sea or from marshy ground is an extremely delicate operation, requiring strengthening treatment in baths of glycerine or paraffin, transport in vacuum chambers, and other measures to ward off the destructive effects of too rapid dehydration. Another urgent first-aid treatment is needed to fix colors in paintings, especially on wood or earthenware.

The problems of conservation and restoration, however, are encountered chiefly during the stage following the excavation. They also arise in the case of monuments surviving in varying conditions

259, 260. *Different approaches to archaeological restoration. Above, ruined site preserved in picturesque surroundings: the Altis at Olympia. Right, complete reconstruction of the Queen's Megaron in the Palace of Knossos, Crete.*

286

COLORPLATE XXVI. *Interior of the Stoa of Attalus in the Agora at Athens. As a reconstruction of an integral part of an ancient site, it forms an unhappy contrast with the adjacent ruins. The aim of the restoration was to house the Agora Museum.*

261. *Isolation of ancient ruins and partial protective restoration: terrace of the Hemicycle in the Temple of Fortuna at Palestrina.*

above ground. It must be understood that the word "restoration" here includes activities of various kinds, for example: (1) measures taken to preserve an archaeological object or structure in the condition in which it has come down to us, protecting it from further damage or alteration; (2) the reassembling of articles discovered in fragments, or of crumbling parts of a building; (3) the partial or total reconstruction of original works, whether architectural or figurative, by replacing the missing parts with modern work. These operations all call for ever-increasing zeal and scientific, cultural, and aesthetic responsibility, and fulfill different needs and purposes. Nevertheless, on the technical level they are all closely connected, and can be considered collectively.

For a long time there has been disagreement among scholars and critics over the principles and methods of restoring monuments and works of art. Conflicting views have been expressed and various solutions suggested according to the different schools of thought at different periods, and in relation to the reasoning or sentiment of individuals, or as a matter of personal taste. These attitudes are also

262, 263. *The Pre-Columbian site of Teotihuacán in Mexico before restoration (left) and after restoration (right).*

reflected in the archaeological field. There was a time when the fascination of antiquity was exerted especially by the Romantic ruin, made glorious by the marks of time and almost reabsorbed into the landscape, a mantle of ivy clinging to the crumbling masonry of its walls, or its columns lying scattered among the rocks or the desert sands. Even today, there is still a widespread instinctive tendency to subordinate or adapt the layout or restoration of archaeological remains to their natural surroundings, or to create a new setting of greenery around them (as at the Altis in Olympia, for example, or the necropolis of Cerveteri). A different approach, more interpretive, deriving its inspiration from the stylistic restoration practiced in nineteenth-century France, aims at re-creating as far as possible the original appearance of ancient monuments, not only by very careful piecing together of the surviving elements (which is how the houses and streets of Pompeii and Herculaneum have been brought back to life), but also sometimes by actually reconstructing whole buildings, even down to the decoration, as in the royal palace at Knossos in Crete, or the Stoa of Attalus in Athens. The complete antithesis of this is the austere viewpoint which maintains, through an excess of scientific scruples, the need to preserve the ruins untouched, exactly as they emerge from the excavations in their confused labyrinths of fallen masonry, without any attempt to carry out even the most obvious reconstructions. Finally, there is the school of thought which, leaving aside all other theories, is occupied exclusively with the preser-

vation of ruins from the attacks of heat, frost, or vegetation, studying the techniques of consolidation by reinforcement of crumbling stonework, injections of cement, the covering over of wall surfaces (for example, the encasing in glass of the great wall of unbaked brick at Gela), or the building of roofs and other protective works. Very often these undertakings, because of the need to avoid the dispersal of fragments, make the reconstruction or the partial restoration of a building advisable or even essential.

One may wonder which of these approaches is ultimately preferable. The most reasonable answer nowadays seems to be a combination of the various methods, according to what is suitable or possible in each case. Sometimes the traditional and impressive aspect of the ruins, set in a traditional landscape, should be preserved. Sometimes excavated structures should be restored or reconstructed. In other cases their protection becomes a matter of urgency. Only the experience, wisdom, good taste, one might even say the honesty, of archaeologists can decide on the choice, fix the limits, or attempt to reconcile the various possible solutions, avoiding abstract or extremist prejudices. No one, indeed, would want to change the appearance of the picturesque ruins of the Palatine or the Baths of Caracalla. But to the excavator of Pompeii and Herculaneum it would seem a crime — indeed, it would be one — not to re-erect the walls, not to reconstruct from minute fragments (with the amazing techniques of the field restorers) the frescoes on walls and ceilings, to rebuild the roofs

264. *Detail of the Greek walls of Gela, Sicily, covered over for protection. The lower part is constructed with blocks of stone and the upper part with rough bricks.*

and re-create the interiors so as to protect them from the elements. They would otherwise have been condemned to the swift and sure destruction which is to be seen in the parts of Pompeii where the earliest excavations took place. Here, however, it was only a matter of rebuilding without guesswork actual fabric broken up by the ancient catastrophe. Very different is the case of the heavy-handed restoration carried out by Sir Arthur Evans at Knossos, where walls, staircases, and wooden columns were totally reconstructed and whole walls repainted, producing the irritating effect of an epic film set created inside the surviving fabric of the venerable monument. What steps should be taken to protect the superb late antique polychrome mosaics of the Roman villa at Piazza Armerina in Sicily, discovered

265. *Protective roofing over some of the mosaics in the late Roman villa at Piazza Armerina in Sicily.*

only a few years ago, and which are among the largest and finest handed down to us from antiquity? How can they be protected from sun and frost and at the same time remain in view, since it would be unthinkable to move them elsewhere? It has even been suggested that the entire villa should be reconstructed — the solution adopted in the Vesuvian cities. But here, clearly, such a colossal architectural fake would have overpowered the genuine beauty of the decorated pavements. They have therefore been provided with an arrangement of light modern coverings, suitable for the protection of the mosaic without spoiling the general appearance of the rest of the monument.

Should antique painting be left on the walls of buildings, or should it be removed to a place of safety in museums? To judge from a com-

266, 267. The method adopted by the Istituto Centrale del Restauro in Rome for removing the paintings from Etruscan tombs. The painted wall surface of a tomb is stripped off in a single piece onto canvas, and the positive is made by transferring it onto another piece of canvas. It is then restored to its original position. Above, paintings from the back wall of the Tomb of the Black Sow at Tarquinii, fourth century B.C., transferred onto canvas and ready to be placed back in position. Below, external structure of a tomb whose paintings have been remounted.

294

*268. The Tomb of the Ship, Tarquinii, fifth century B.C. The paintings removed from the walls and the ceiling have been transferred onto canvas and rearranged in order to re-create the interior of a typical tomb. Museum, Tarquinii.*

parison between the frescoes removed from Pompeii and Herculaneum in the eighteenth century and preserved in the museum at Naples, unharmed and as fresh as the day they were painted, and those discovered only a few decades ago in the Via dell'Abbondanza in Pompeii and now reduced to little more than shadows, the decision should be in favor of the tricky operation of detaching them. But in situations where it is possible to reconstruct the interiors, the wall decorations can and should be left in their original positions. In the case of Etruscan tomb paintings, too, it seems pointless to argue over abstract theories — whether, in other words, the definite safety of removal is preferable to the living effect of the painting with the brilliance of its color preserved by the humidity in the original evocative setting of the hypogeum. Logic demands that anything not threatened with decay (through the action of nitric salts, vegetable or animal agencies, or the extreme fragility of the rock) should be left where it is, and that painted surfaces in immediate danger should be removed. The technique of this kind of salvage work now in use has been perfected by the Istituto Centrale del Restauro in Rome; it is carried out by peeling off a very thin film of color and plaster in a continuous sheet from entire walls onto rolls of cloth, and then transferring it onto frames, which make it possible to reconstruct the layout of the tomb. Since 1950, some famous series of paintings have

269, 270. Restored statues and bronzes. Left, marble copy of an Amazon by Phidias. It was discovered in the Canopus at Hadrian's Villa, Tivoli, and reconstructed from the fragments without any modern additions. Museum, Hadrian's Villa. Below, large Greek bronze krater with ornamental figures discovered in a tomb at Vix near Châtillon-sur-Seine, France, and restored in the Louvre laboratories. Sixth century B.C. Museum, Châtillon-sur-Seine.

COLORPLATE XXVII. *Detail of the Canopus of Hadrian's Villa, Tivoli. It has been partly restored, and copies have replaced the original statues.*

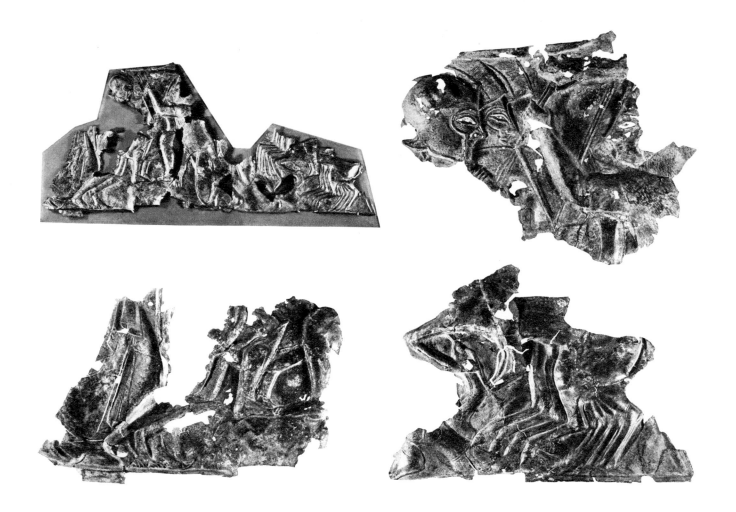

271-74. Bronze sheet representing the fight between Hercules and Cycnus. The first illustration shows the sheet following reconstruction and restoration, and the others show details of the sheet as it appeared when it was found. Archaeological Museum, Perugia.

275. Spectroscopic photograph of an ancient bronze (fragments of the chariot of Chianciano).

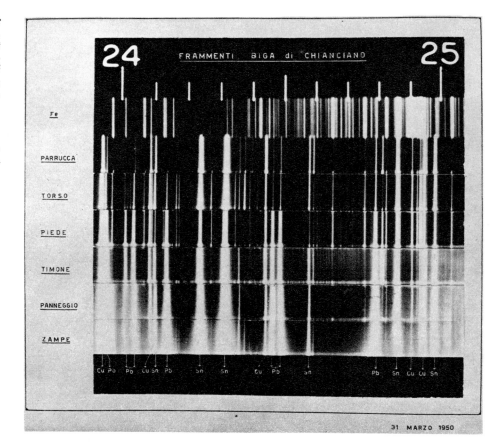

276. *Example of an early museum. The Rotunda of the Museo Pio Clementino in the Vatican, built for Pius VI by M. Simonetti at the end of the eighteenth century.*

been removed from the tombs of Tarquinii, including those known as the Tomb of the Chariots, the Tomb of the Triclinium, the Tomb of the Funeral Couch, the Tomb of the Olympiads, etc. The risky method of cutting a section out of the wall (as was done in the last century for the François Tomb at Vulci) has been superseded; in the case of mural frescoes, the removing of a layer of plaster is preferable. Similar techniques — cutting out and framing, or lifting in a single layer — are nowadays used for mosaics.

The problem of the restoration and completion of works of plastic art, especially sculpture, is particularly delicate, both in principle and in practice. As we know, during the Renaissance and the seventeenth century whole antique statues were built up without scruple, often

277. The Victory of Samothrace in the Louvre. The arrangement of this part of the museum was begun under the Second Empire and completed in 1933.

from mutilated remains or fragments, to agree with the prevailing conception of a living antiquity, and of the work of art as an ornament rather than an object of study. Later, strict historical methodology led to the opposite extreme: the added arms, hands, heads, or noses were removed, in order to restore the antique piece to the condition in which it had actually survived. Some museums seemed to become collections of anatomical specimens. Nowadays there is usually a more balanced compromise between the requirements of accuracy and enjoyment of the unaltered original, and the need to preserve to some extent an understanding of the work of art as a whole, suggesting its form and where possible reducing the unpleasing effect of damaged or missing pieces. An excellent example

301

of this kind of work is the recent restoration, already referred to, of the Laocoön — a work which has long occupied an important position in the history of the changing attitudes to the restoration of antique sculpture.

At this point may be mentioned the work of conservation and restoration carried out on other types of objects and minor works of art: ceramics, bronze articles and statuettes, goldsmiths' work, coins, ivories, and decorated bone. Apart from their documentary value and their intrinsic aesthetic worth, such things form the "daily bread" of the restorers (far more so than great works of painting and sculpture), and therefore qualify for special attention on the part of technicians and laboratories. In fact, in their case the day of experimental methods has gone. The problem of restoring metal objects is particularly absorbing, especially where bronzes are concerned. These are usually cleaned by mechanical methods, according to circumstances. Great care has to be exercised to avoid destroying the surface patina, and the subsequent wax polishing must also be reduced to a minimum. There are also ways of reducing oxidation growths by

302

COLORPLATE XXVIII. *The central hall of the Egyptian Museum, Cairo, with the group of Amenhotep III and Queen Tiy. The museum was built between 1895 and 1900 by Marcel-Lazare Dourgnon and opened in 1902.*

279. *The north wing of the Gela Museum, built by Franco Minissi in 1958.*

means of solvent baths of distilled water, oxalic acid, etc. — always providing, of course, that enough of the original metal survives in an uncrystallized condition. Where fragments of thin sheets of metal have to be pieced together, gesso is used both as a foundation and for making good missing areas. More recently, a binding made of powdered metal has been used in preference. Special chemical strengthening agents are being tried out in various ways for the conservation of ivories, bone, wood, leather, fabrics, and papyrus.

The final subject to be considered is the assembling and display of archaeological material in museums. As regards the architecture, layout, and equipment of museums in general, and more particularly museums of art and antiquities, a vast amount of thought and study has been devoted in the last few years to this subject, generally known as museography. Leaving aside tradition and the relationship between private and public collections, the planning of a truly modern and functional archaeological museum is nowadays a question of urgent interest. In particular, there are discussions as to whether a museum should be simply a place where antique objects

280. The reserve collection of the Archaeological Museum in Ferrara, containing objects from the necropolis of Spina in the course of classification and reorganization. One of the most serious and pressing problems of archaeological museums is the storage of material not on show.

are kept, so that these are more or less all on view and accessible (as in the crowded rooms and showcases of some of the old collections, or in closed and selective collections of private origin — the Museo Barracco in Rome, for example, or small local antiquarian museums), or whether the general public should be shown a more or less restricted choice of single masterpieces, keeping the rest in reserve for purposes of study. When it comes to arranging the exhibits, there are several conflicting systems — chronological, typological, or geographical. Some favor the concentration of material from a wide area in large national establishments; others prefer decentralization in small local museums. One aspect of modernization takes the form of the introduction of abundant information (written notes, tables, dioramas, plans, photographs, reconstructions), after the model of a documentary type of museum such as the Musée de l'Homme (prehistoric and ethnographical) in Paris. Modernization also appears in the simplified and functional style of the architecture, furniture, showcases, stands, and lighting arrangements. The difference between old and new museums can be judged if one compares traditional and unchanged foundations of the eighteenth or nineteenth centuries, such as the Vatican Museum, with typical recent creations like the one at Gela in Sicily, or if one observes the results of the modernization carried out, or still in progress, of large overcrowded collections of antiquities like those of the Villa Giulia in Rome, or of Saint-Germain-en-Laye.

A rational solution of these problems can be reached in each case

*281, 282. Special aspects of archaeological museums. Left, reconstruction of the interior of the tomb of the painter Meie from Deir el-Medineh, near Thebes. End of the Eighteenth Dynasty. Egyptian Museum, Turin. Right, Viking ship from Oseberg, tenth century A.D., now in the Oslo Museum.*

only if we bear in mind all the essentials and functions of an archaeological museum, which are: (1) the basic requirements of conservation, security, space, and room for expansion for the collection; (2) its function as a center of study, which calls for the easy accessibility of all the collections to those interested, together with the presence of laboratories, photographic archives, etc.; (3) its cultural, educational, and instructive role for the general public and for tourists; (4) the " history " of the museum itself, as evidence of a phase of culture, which imposes serious limitations on the alteration of certain traditional arrangements. It is obvious that large museums can provide better conditions and certain subsidiary services for study and work. But it is also clear that a selective and up-to-date display of material arranged in an informative way, and the development of museums near the places where the objects they contain were discovered (or near archaeological zones), would lead to a much better understanding of local history and art on the part of the general public, and would encourage the tourist industry to spread to new areas. The number of objects exhibited, however, should not be so few as to inconvenience scholars, and in any case there should be easily accessible and well-arranged storerooms — which is not always the case. An expedient frequently used (though it is not an entirely satisfactory or complete solution) is the opening of single sections of the museum in turn to the public. The architectural setting and layout of newly created or entirely rebuilt museums (in cases, that is, where regard for the existing surroundings or for tra-

ditional arrangements are not against it) should be planned exclusively with a view to setting off the antiquities and the theme of the collection as simply as possible and with the minimum amount of pretention. Least of all should the architects and interior designers use the museum as an opportunity for indulging their own personal tastes, as has sometimes happened in recent years. A much greater freedom of grouping and boldness of layout is permissible in temporary archaeological and artistic exhibitions, which are now becoming more and more frequent, and which contribute greatly to the spread of culture — and often to the advancement of learning as well.

Finally, particular attention should be drawn to the specialized museums, because of both their interest and their problems. These are concerned with the conservation of special categories of objects and monuments, such as collections of coins and medals, epigraphical collections, open-air architectural museums, naval museums like that at Nemi, and the purely teaching collections of scientific institutions and universities, among which the collections of plaster casts from antique sculpture are of particular interest because of their traditional character. These last have played a major part in the growth and teaching of the "archaeology of art." The one in Berlin was especially celebrated; nowadays the most important one belongs to the University of Rome.

## Illustration and interpretation of archaeological data: archaeology as a historical discipline

The archaeological cycle which we have followed from the initial planning and equipment, through exploration, the collection of data, and the conservation of finds, is brought to completion by its final stages: illustration and interpretation. It can be seen that all the activities described so far belong only to the first stage of archaeology as a historical discipline: to the period of *observation*, to which the logical successors are the illustrative stage or *description*, and the interpretative stage or true *history*. This division of the process into three — offered with reservations, of course, and allowing for the fact that there is always an element of the approximate in every simplified outline — seems justified by the actual course followed by archaeological studies, particularly during the last hundred years, their characteristics and their relationship with the humanities in general. Nowadays, it no longer seems possible to conceive of archaeology as a separate discipline from history, whether "history of art," or "prehistory," or the "history of culture" or "ethnology" or "cultural anthropology" of antiquity, since all these lines of study converge each in their turn on history. Nor can its function be limited simply to the collection of material. It is clear that the activities of archaeologists, varied according to personal preferences, range from active research in the field to the classification and systematic publication of monuments and discoveries (sometimes called the "philology" of archaeological studies), and thence to the formulation of critical hypotheses and histories of ancient arts and cultures. An analogous process can be observed in other parallel and similar fields of knowledge. For example, in the study of ancient literary sources, where it is represented by the examination of texts, philological and linguistic analysis, and finally the history of literature, thought, and institutions; or in the field of cultural anthropology, where one can distinguish the successive stages of documentary research, descriptive ethnography, and finally true historical ethnology.

Archaeological material as such — the artifacts and monuments of antiquity, the results of discoveries, the material assembled in museums — acquire significance and attain their full value only through the unfolding of the entire process, from the initial discovery to its final illustration and interpretation. Without this, they would remain mere curiosities. It can therefore be said that any excavation not followed up by study and publication is devoid of any scientific value, and in the long run is equivalent to the actual destruction of sources of information. This is true not only of unauthorized searches carried out in the old way with the sole aim of collecting objects or as a form of looting, but also of official excavations speeded up by the natural enthusiasm of the archaeologists (or sometimes through necessity) to the point where study of the finds cannot keep pace with them. Nowadays this happens all too often in the countries richest in antiquities, such as Italy. The need for description (i. e., the second stage of the archaeological process) therefore becomes, particularly in our own day, of the utmost importance and urgency.

Where the publication of new discoveries is concerned, it is necessary on the one hand that the information should promptly be made available for the rapid dissemination of knowledge, and on the other that the data should be accurate and complete, particularly with regard to the illustrations (photographs, plans, drawings). These two requirements cannot always be reconciled, and this may give rise to delays because of the scruples of the author, or may lead to the circulation of interesting archaeological information at a merely journalistic level. Technically, the problem is often solved by the publication of an interim report by the scholar in charge of the research shortly after the completion of his work, or annually in the case of a series of excavations (known as a preliminary report), which can then be followed up by the complete and definitive publication of the results and the material discovered, systematically and fully presented. These sometimes take the form of monographs in several volumes devoted to the topography, the monuments, and the individual categories of works of art and objects from the site, edited by various scholars who are specialists in the different fields. Most of the minor discoveries are made known through periodicals and bulletins; the overall picture of archaeological events in general, or those in individual countries or particular areas of study, can be followed in the news bulletins or under particular headings in the main specialist journals, or in the appropriate publications.

Another aspect of the publishing of archaeological monuments and material concerns the preparation of monographs on single regions or localities (independently of any particular investigation or series of investigations), the publication of museum catalogues, and the systematic assembling of typologically related works of art, objects, and documents. This last type of work enjoyed a tremendous vogue in the nineteenth century, being congenial to the principles of a matter-of-fact and analytical type of scholarship. In a way it provided the solid foundation for every kind of comparative research, whether in the form of a *corpus* (intended to be complete) of the known examples of individual archaeological categories, or as series of short monographs on works of art with constant characteristics (for example, *Denkmäler griechischer und römischer Skulptur*, published by H. Brunn, P. Arndt, and F. Bruckmann from 1888 onward, or the *Corpus Vasorum Antiquorum*, a work of international collaboration, from 1922 on). The epigraphical collections were, and still are, of special importance in their own field; they include works such as the *Corpus Inscriptionum Latinarum*, founded by T. Mommsen in 1863. But at the

*284. Museums as places of learning and study. Gallery of casts at the Istituto di Archeologia at the University of Rome.*

present time the rapid increase in the number of discoveries, and the ever more exacting requirements of scientific publication, are making things progressively more difficult for the scholars and institutes responsible for continuing these works. The result is that the rate of publication of some of the great *corpora* is slowing down, and little by little they are being replaced by more manageable periodical lists.

Information concerning the monuments, archaeological material, and various phenomena of ancient civilizations also appears in publications of a practical nature, such as manuals, encyclopedias, and dictionaries, collections of plates, and classified bibliographies. The latter are constantly growing in size — both those of a general nature and those concerned with some particular period, civilization, or type of material. They may take the form of appendices to periodicals, or of independent volumes. In fact, they are becoming an increasingly indispensable guide to scholars, now that the volume of scientific literature is increasing at such an alarming pace. It is next to impossible nowadays for any single researcher to follow and to check everything which is being discovered and published, not only in connection with his own subject and field of interest in general but even concerning the investigation of highly specialized problems.

Archaeology, like every other historical discipline, and indeed like

*285. The library of the Istituto Archeologico Germanico in Rome, one of the oldest and most famous centers for archaeological study in the world.*

practically every other science, is at present in a state of crisis whose outcome is difficult to foresee — precisely because of the difficulty in acquiring sufficiently specialized knowledge as well as adequate breadth in the field of study. The problem is that of overspecialization, which arises not simply because of some whim or fashion on the part of scholars, or a progressive narrowing of outlook, but because of the enormous accumulation of scientific data and the continual advances in methods of investigation. At the present moment, an archaeologist who has specialized in the study of Greek pottery would find it difficult (with the possible exception of Sir John Beazley, with his universal eye and mind) to feel equally at home among the archaic pottery of Corinth and that of Athens, or to be as familiar with Attic red-figure ceramics of the fourth century as with those of the fifth century. At the same time, because of our increasing awareness of the interdependence of historical factors, which calls for a breaking down of the old distinctions of nineteenth-century classification, we feel more and more the need for a wider outlook. We realize that it is impossible to grasp any single artistic or cultural phenomenon if not only the related areas but the general framework of the history and civilization to which it belongs are disregarded or unknown. In other words, if it is true to say that analysis is simple and straightforward, and synthesis is difficult if not impossible, it is equally true to say that a critically valid analysis cannot be separated from a certain degree of synthesis. These statements may seem obvious and vague, but they apply in a concrete, not to say a dramatic, fashion to the work of research, classification, study, and publication in the field of archaeology.

As far as its scientific organization is concerned, archaeology is now divided into numerous widely differing branches, according to the periods, localities, or spheres of influence of the ancient civilizations being studied, or according to the specific character of the monuments, documents, or phenomena under examination. We have come a long way from the single, limited, nineteenth-century "archaeology of art" concerned almost exclusively with the classical world. Prehistoric archaeologists, for example, already tend to be divided into those concerned with primitive (i. e., paleolithic) man, trained primarily in the natural sciences, and those studying the more recent prehistoric cultures, and European and Asiatic protohistory (i. e., the neolithic, bronze, and iron ages up to the Middle Ages), with their own clearly defined approach and traditions of study. Ethnological archaeologists devote their attention to the origins of non-European cultures, and include specialists in American Pre-Columbian archaeology. Orientalists are working on various aspects of the ancient civilizations of the Near and Middle East (Egyptologists, Assyriologists, Iranists, etc.) and those of Central Asia, India, China, Japan, etc. Classical archaeologists are concerned with the Graeco-Roman world and its sphere of influence. Christian and medieval archaeologists form yet another specialized category. Furthermore, alongside the more general fields of the archaeologists who study ancient monuments and various types of antique objects as historians of culture or as art historians, often concentrating on architecture, figurative works of art, bronzes, or ceramics, we find specialist topographical archaeologists, who study places, settlements, lines of communication, and whose activities are nowadays greatly assisted by such modern means as aerial photography. There are also archaeologists who devote themselves to the study of written documents or inscriptions (epigraphers), or the study of coins (numismatists), from the point of view of their historical, social, or linguistic interest. It should be emphasized once again, however, that to lay too much stress on the divisions between these various sectors would conflict with the need for an overall understanding of the characteristics and growth of the ancient civilizations — and is often also incompatible with the practical demands of research.

An obvious means of overcoming the problem of the conflict between specialization and co-ordination is to be found in the organization of research and studies. Scientific bodies do exist (and are, happily, on the increase) which facilitate contact between archaeologists on a national and an international level. There is a constantly increasing amount of collaboration or team work (to which students of the humanities, unlike those of the physical and natural sciences, do not always take kindly, and there are profitable meetings, conferences, and congresses. University teaching, however, plays the most important part of all in providing future archaeologists with a complete preparation, not only in the many and varied fields of their own professional discipline, but also in the collateral studies of history, literature, the history of thought, sociology, and even, where possible, the natural sciences and technology. More and more the main task of the university seems to be not so much to encourage specialization on the part of the young at the student level by a multiplication of "special subjects" corresponding to the areas of study listed above (every real scholar will inevitably become a specialist all too soon), as to lay down and encourage a course of comprehensive and dynamic studies for the archaeologist. In this way the university truly assumes the character of a school — i. e., a living and continuous tradition of knowledge.

The evaluation of archaeological data may seem a separate and distinct stage — the third and final step in the process of our studies — but in fact it is often already present, potentially or explicitly, in the description of material or the publication of finds. These are seldom put forward as a simple presentation of material data and of figures without some attempt at selection, putting them in their context and forming a judgment. It may even be said that scholars concerned with historical aspects can, and should, suggest the actual basis of the initial research in the case of scientifically planned excavations, provided that it does not take the form of a preconceived theory to be demonstrated or refuted, which would hinder or impair

315

the freedom of the work and the objectivity of the observations. (Fanatical archaeologists have even been known to try to minimize or conceal discoveries which conflicted with their own theories.) The progress of knowledge and ideas has made it possible to recognize many phenomena which could have been known at an earlier stage, had the material been clearly understood; Mycenaean Greece is a case in point. This explains the frequency of "chain" discoveries starting off at a particular moment. The fundamental value of the archaeologist as a historian depends on the precise degree of promptness, sensitivity, and above all impartiality with which he reacts to anything new, however slight, turned up by discoveries and excavations, modifying his own earlier impressions or even reversing, if necessary, his own convictions and theories. In this way, archaeology supplements the method of historical reconstruction by a process all its own, which could be described as dynamic in that the critical reasoning is continually and progressively renewed with the changing factors — i. e., the material evidence.

The interpretation of archaeological evidence, through a long and distinguished tradition of scholarship, has as we know contributed decisively to the reconstruction of the outlines of the history, civilization, and history of art of the peoples of the ancient world. Of course, where classical antiquity is concerned, archaeology runs parallel to the written tradition, which occupies an important place not only as regards our knowledge of history in the narrow sense, but also in connection with the history of civilization and the history of art. Many of the ideas and values of Greek art would escape us if we did not have the works of Pliny and Pausanias. For the ancient East as well it is the written documents (even if of archaeological provenance) which give us the main outlines of thought and historical development. One might well ask what use "pure" archaeology would be, with only the language of stones, objects, or carved and painted representation to go by, and no help from written documents or transmitted memories, in reconstructing even a minimally authentic image of a past which vanished thousands of years ago, and of the lives, relationships, and thoughts of the men who created it. How much would we know about the Greeks and Romans without classical literature, or about the Egyptians and Babylonians without the papyri or the inscribed clay tablets? How much have we effectively learned — how much will we ever learn — of the inhabitants of Europe in the bronze age and the early iron age, of the neolithic farmers and shepherds of Eurasia, let alone the primeval hunters of the long and far distant ice ages?

Theoretically, one could give a negative answer to this solemn question, from the strictly scientific and philosophical viewpoint, since the flotsam and jetsam from the immense shipwreck of time only helps to conjure up fleeting distorted shadows, reflecting our own imagination and trains of thought rather than images of a vanished past. But archaeologists refuse to accept such a discouraging

COLORPLATE XXIX. *The Colossi of Memnon commanding the Nile Valley at Thebes.*
*These huge statues were erected by Amenhotep II (1405-1370 B.C.) in front of his*
*funeral temple. Even in antiquity they symbolized the mysteries of the past. At dawn*
*one of them would send forth a sound which was thought to be the groan of the dying*
*Ethiopian hero Memnon to his mother, Eos.*

conclusion, and believe that it is possible, with the help of tangible evidence, to work out a reconstruction of the ways of life and social organizations of ancient peoples, to distinguish to some extent their cultural and ethnological groups, to outline the phases of their development and decline, to identify the various influences at work, and even to trace migrations, conquests, and similar activities.

Of course, in many cases one is limited to hypotheses, in which the subjective and personal views of the interpreters, together with prevailing theories and the attitudes of different schools, play a large part. Insuperable limits are obviously imposed by the level of specific and general knowledge at the time the hypotheses were formulated. These should therefore always be regarded as provisional and subject to modification, development, or elaboration. The risk of error in conclusions based entirely, or almost entirely, on archaeological data seems all the greater when we remember, for example, that there exist races, cultures, and religions which can be documented from the historical and ethnological point of view, and which are destined to vanish or die without leaving even the slightest trace of any monumental remains. We know that very different cultural and artistic phenomena can appear in the same place at very brief intervals of time and even contemporaneously, depending on social currents and backgrounds. (Even in our own day, for example, there are some countries where one can see in use carts with solid wheels, of a type dating back many thousands of years, and at the same time modern television sets.) On the other hand, there are inventions and traditions which are common to areas and peoples a great distance apart; and the movement of influences from one country to another does not necessarily mean that the second was conquered by the first, or was invaded. Greece in the second century B.C., for instance, did not conquer Rome but, on the contrary, was conquered by the latter, and the *chinoiseries* of the seventeenth and eighteenth centuries do not mean that there was a migration of Chinese into Europe! Many of the historical, ethnographical, and stylistic outlines laid down by modern archaeology are, in effect, based on the erroneous concept of an automatic correspondence between material forms of ancient civilizations and historical facts. (It has even been stated, in the famous "law of Kossinna," that every variation in surviving artifacts proclaims the existence of a different people.) In addition, these outlines have often been built up from such ludicrously sparse and fragmentary evidence — especially in areas where archaeological research has hardly begun — that they should be regarded, as a matter of common sense, not merely as imperfect and approximate, but even almost certainly false.

All this is not intended to imply that the efforts so far made to reconstruct the outlines of the far distant past from the surviving material evidence are not legitimate and appreciable, and have not achieved substantially positive results. It only means that constant vigilance is necessary in the critical evaluation of available data, combined with a sensitive appreciation of historical problems and a wealth of experience transcending the limits of specialized knowledge, however profound, of the particular archaeological material which one is trying to interpret. History is indeed, by its very nature, global. It makes use of the concurrence of a multiplicity of tools and the most varied disciplines. Thus, the archaeologist who proposes to reconstruct at least a part of the historical reality which lies hidden in the monumental remains and objects of a particular period or a particular cultural area should take into account at the same time not only his immediate object of study (i. e., artifacts in the context of their geographical surroundings, considered in their chronological succession, the analysis of their forms, functions, and styles), but also the possible help, direct or indirect, of the literary traditions and written sources, the linguistic and ethnological sciences, not to mention historical analogy — i. e., the elementary method, all too often neglected, of drawing parallels between the events of an obscure or nebulous past and those of epochs and civilizations historically well known, and even of the present day. It is on these foundations that modern archaeology is progressively conquering newer and firmer territory for our knowledge of the history of humanity.

# PRESENT PROBLEMS AND
# FUTURE PROSPECTS

### *Archaeology in the modern world: misunderstandings and dangers*

Now that we have reached the end of our journey through all the vicissitudes, the strange discoveries, the triumphs and experiences of man's exploration of the past, we must not forget the concluding point — the significance of all this complex of activities in relation to modern society and its contribution to progress.

Let us first of all sum up the present situation and examine its problems. As we already know, archaeology has played an increasingly important part, not only in the field of scholarship, but also in cultural and, to some extent, even in economic affairs in the contemporary world. Furthermore, official circles have definitely accepted the concept that archaeological research is a branch of science, both in methods and aims, and that ancient remains — monuments and excavated objects — are irreplaceable documents for the knowledge of history, and must be protected and given full value as a precious heritage of our civilization. It cannot be claimed, however, that these principles are generally accepted by the general public, even in the most enlightened countries, or that they are universally applied without resistance.

It must even be stated that people in general, regardless of class or education, still have on the whole only a superficial understanding of archaeology, vaguely emotional in character, and very similar to that prevailing in earlier times. The popular interest in archaeological problems seems to be chiefly nourished by the old motives — the fascination of mystery, the lure of the unforeseen, the excitement of discovery, the buried treasure, the appeal of fabulous worlds — all of which have an immediate effect on the imagination. Hence the enormous success in recent years of a certain kind of romantic archaeological literature. But this attitude also gives rise to a whole series of prejudices, convictions, and forms of behavior which have been mentioned several times in the course of the preceding chapters. Among these are a failure to understand the value of ancient remains and archaeological objects as documents and scientific data, considering only their interest as curiosities, in some cases their pleasing aesthetic quality, and above all their monetary value; and the deeply rooted instinctive belief, amounting to an unshakable conviction, that excavating, and collecting and dealing in antiquities, are the concern of the individual dilettante and of private enterprise, in much the same way as games and field sports, or the buying and selling of ordinary merchandise. As a result, there is an equally instinctive tendency to make unfavorable comparisons between archaeological remains and their study and conservation (regarded as "recreational" and "nonessential"), and more serious matters such as economic requirements, the increased needs of building and industry, and the like.

It may be argued that there has existed for some time, and in nearly every country, legislation tending to the opposite view, which, far from supporting the attitude of the general public, positively condemns some of its manifestations. Nevertheless, we should not delude ourselves into believing that the very extensive protective legislation of the modern states, though it is continually increasing in range and power, can really provide complete protection, even within the often narrow limits of its right of direct intervention. It has already been pointed out that there is a considerable (and, unfortunately, constantly increasing) amount of illegal activity, especially in Italy. There is no doubt that it is carried on chiefly by speculators, clandestine excavators, those who buy up excavated objects, middlemen, agents, big antique dealers, and in the last analysis the purchasers, whether native or foreign, who are aware of the illegality involved and therefore operate more or less in secret. It can also be stated that the impunity enjoyed by these operators is due to deficiencies in the law itself and to the meagerness of sanctions, or the lack of supervision and failure to report offenses.

At the root of all these evils, however — the ease with which organized plunder is carried out, and the innumerable thoughtless violations of the archaeological patrimony — is the prevailing utter failure to appreciate the motives which inspire the laws relating to antiquities. Respectable citizens who would not steal a pin, and who would think it a crime to damage the flowerbeds in a public garden, have no scruples whatever about acquiring archaeological objects from illicit excavators, or having an ancient wall destroyed with all possible speed if it should happen to be encountered in the course of building work or agriculture. The smuggling of antiquities is looked on with the same indulgence as the smuggling of cigarettes. There is clearly no perception of what a serious loss to historical knowledge may be caused by the dispersal of material found in association in a tomb secretly pillaged, or the disappearance of the traces of even the least significant of ruins. Even the public authorities and tribunals, so zealous in suppressing fiscal offenses or those against propriety, generally seem more or less indifferent to damage to their archaeological heritage, and thus reflect the common tendency to dismiss this material as useless extravagance. In this way their attitude also contributes to the weakening of the legal protective measures.

The dangers which beset ancient monuments and archaeological sites have become particularly acute in recent years, because of the progress of technology and general economic expansion, resulting in an increase in urban and rural building, industrial installations, road construction, hydraulic schemes, harbor works, and intensive agriculture. This phenomenon is particularly marked in regions at a comparatively low stage of development, such as the Mediterranean lands, the Near and Middle East, Southeast Asia, and Latin America — in fact, just where archaeological evidence is most plentiful. The demands of modern living cannot be resisted, and bring about the rapid destruction of antique remains. Landscapes, ruins, and burial grounds which have remained undisturbed for centuries are now turned upside down in the course of a few months. For example, since World War II the agrarian reforms in Italy have transformed the appearance of the marshlands of Lazio and Tuscany, endangering the riches concealed in their earth with the destructive power of the tractors. Until then, many of its regions had remained as wild as when they were seen and described by Dennis in the Romantic period. In Apulia, traces of prehistoric dwellings revealed only a few years ago by aerial photography have now disappeared. The sudden surge of private and industrial building, especially along the coast, is causing such rapid and extensive destruction that it is impossible even to record the monuments before they vanish — a deplorable state of affairs which also threatens Mediterranean Spain. No need to recall the flooding of the Nile Valley for hundreds of miles in Egyptian Nubia and the Sudan through the building of the new Aswan Dam. The tragedy lies mainly in the fact that these developments are so sudden and intensive that they catch us almost everywhere unprepared. They are taking place just where facilities are lacking or inadequate. Even where there were sufficient means to deal with any normal situation, these are unable to cope with the present emergency. World-wide appeals in support of salvage operations are little more than a token gesture, like a few drops of water in a desert. Truly, we cannot conceal from ourselves that, just when archaeological research has reached the highest point of development and technical perfection, an unprecedented threat of destruction appears to menace the tangible remains from the past, striking at the very roots of this research. World archaeology is, in substance, facing a serious crisis, and it is impossible to see beyond the present problems and remedial measures to the ultimate consequences.

## Can archaeology be reconciled with the growth of modern society?

Today it appears more necessary and urgent than ever to mobilize all the available forces of culture, at a national and an international level, to try to clarify ideas concerning the aims and needs of archaeology, to find a way of reconciling these needs with the various demands of modern life, and to tackle the immediate problems.

The first task to be undertaken is largely informative and educational — to increase general awareness (still, I repeat, very limited) of the scientific importance of archaeological researches and of the irreplaceable value of the information provided by finds. It is not only, or even primarily, a question of making the inquiring or enthusiastic public and the responsible authorities see that ancient remains and objects, whatever they may be, should be treated with special respect. It must be universally realized that a stretch of Roman road or a prehistoric shard can have the same interest as an old parchment, an incunabulum, early records, even the tobacco jar once owned by a famous person. And dispersal, theft, or destruction in this field must be regarded not simply as damage to property, but as an attack on the historical patrimony of the human race. It should be stressed in an unequivocal fashion that all investigations and discoveries, all archaeological activities, the conservation of monuments, the collecting of relics from the past, are important not only for the pleasure they give, the dedicated enthusiasm they inspire, the aesthetic satisfaction to be derived from them. What counts above all is scholarship, directed toward the final and supreme objective: historical knowledge. This means — and we cannot repeat it too often, even to ourselves — that any excavation where details of the discovery, the association of the material, etc., are even partially neglected has failed in its purpose, however great the quantity of splendid sculpture or exquisite pottery unearthed. To form a collection or a museum with objects assembled haphazard and of uncertain provenance is a pursuit which has nothing to do with the progress of learning; and, on the other hand, the harm caused by the unavoidable destruction of architectural remains or the dispersal of finds belonging to a particular complex (a tomb or a votive hoard) can be minimized by the existence of an accurate record of the find, with notes, photographs, and other documentation, and by the publication of such a record.

This last remark indicates, if I am not mistaken, the possibilities that exist of reconciling archaeological needs with the other interests of contemporary society. Archaeologists are not fanatical Utopians who demand — or would even desire — the complete conservation of every single material trace of antiquity at the cost of immobilizing the activities of modern life. Clearly it is a question of proportion, and decisions must depend not only on external pressures but, at an even earlier stage, on the quantity and nature of the remains. For example, it would patently be absurd to fill museums with heaps of tile fragments picked up on the surface or excavated on the site of an ancient city. It is always possible to estimate relative degrees of importance before permitting a piece of destruction or deciding its extent. The really important thing is to insure that there be no loss or destruction of any useful information concerning the topography, history, chronology, or culture of the archaeological sites, and the development of the cultures which are documented in them. The principles of modern scientific archaeology, already stated more than once, demand that exact records be kept, since these are more important than the objects themselves; and it is precisely on the safeguarding of such data that a truly uncompromising effort must be concentrated. The distinction may seem a subtle one (and it is not always perfectly clear even to professional archaeologists, let alone laymen), but it sums up an attitude of fundamental importance for the establishment of rules of conduct, both in law and in fact, concerning the relationship of archaeology with the outside world. Indeed, the claim that valuable scientific data should not be destroyed, and that such data should be voluntarily passed on to qualified persons (in substance, a demand for full scientific control of archaeological discoveries), does not seem, in theory at least, irreconcilable with the needs of modern society—provided always that the public have or acquire good standards of civic behavior, and that, moreover, vexatious interference, bureaucratic tiresomeness, and fiscal restrictions are entirely eliminated.

It is clear that scientific ends of archaeology cannot be safeguarded by a private enterprise system which would leave investigations, the collecting of antiquities, their ownership, and the trade in them to be governed by the wishes and interests of individual citizens, as used to be the case — and still is, to a considerable extent, in some countries. (Where the laws are more severe, clandestine speculation attempts to maintain the same system illegally.) One has only to remember the excavations carried out by untrained and unskilled workers, the impossibility of supervising such activities or intervening, the difficulties in the way of learning about the finds and insuring their publication, as well as the innumerable losses and dispersals of material. But even a system based on the principle of State ownership of the subsoil and the complete regulation of archaeological activities, such as exists in Italy, is not without its drawbacks. The provisions of the laws, and their application, may tend to lay too much emphasis on the administrative and fiscal aspects of protection and preservation, at the expense of the cultural and scientific ones. The State is often inclined to concentrate on the protection of its "property," thus ultimately putting itself on the same level as the illegal private speculation it is combatting. In other words, it is judging antique objects by their material value. This conflict of opposing economic interests encourages the whole clandestine traffic in antiquities, which does so much harm to the primary interests of scientific supervision. One wonders whether a really ideal system of protective legislation in the archaeological field would not be along the lines of an absolute guarantee of immunity for private citizens laying information leading to the official recovery and publishing of finds, coupled with a certain amount of latitude as regards the ownership and circulation of antique objects, not even excluding the possibility that some of the State-owned archaeological material at present lying about unseen in museum storerooms be put on the market — provided, of course, that it has first been published scientifically.

The safeguarding of the archaeological heritage would be much more effective if there were any guarantee of adequate financial means. Here, again, we come up against the problem of the failure of public opinion to appreciate values of this kind — public opinion meaning the ruling classes, parliaments, governments, and even, in the last analysis, State budgets. Even in countries where the technical services available for antiquities have a long and glorious tradition, as in Italy, such services now seem inadequate for their task, particularly in the present state of emergency — either through shortage of staff, lack of funds, or out-of-date and unsuitable systems of administrative control which reduce still further their already limited field of operation, or even paralyze their activities altogether. We have to recognize that the slight progress achieved in combatting the dangers of a state of affairs already leading to disastrous results is entirely due to the faith, moral courage, and sincere personal devotion of the archaeologists who direct these bodies or belong to them. Clearly, what is needed in this field is a much vaster and more decisive program of reform than can be effected by a cautious bureaucratic adoption of small innovations, and one which will take into account the purely economic value of the benefits accruing to the State from its archaeological and monumental patrimony — particularly through the tourist industry.

### The need for co-ordination of archaeological research and studies

Even inside the field of professional archaeology there is not always a clear understanding of the importance and interrelationship of the various operations which make up the cycle of research and study already described (teaching, equipping, reconnaissance and excavation, conservation, publication), and of the essential principle that each of these activities is subordinate to the ultimate aim — the progress of historical knowledge. We know that some archaeologists are more suited by temperament and training to practical tasks, while others prefer work of a mainly speculative nature. Some devote themselves to active exploration on the site, others to the running of museums, schools, and the like. It is only human nature that each should have an affection for his own particular branch of the profession, and attribute special importance to it; the essential thing is to preserve an awareness of the interdependence of all these activities and the necessity for constant collaboration among them.

It cannot be denied, for example, that the enthusiasm aroused by archaeology and the fascination it exercises in its never-ending pursuit of new discoveries is often reflected, naturally enough, in the outlook and plans of militant archaeologists, however serious and scholarly, who encourage an expansion of their program of excavation not only beyond the practical need for chance finds and the continuation of major archaeological undertakings in places of world-wide interest, but sometimes even beyond the requirements of serious scientific programs and beyond the capacity of the facilities available for conservation and study. Along with this "digging mania," which affects specialists as well as amateurs, goes a regrettably widespread tendency to delay publishing the results of investigations, sometimes for many years, until it is too late to be of any use, and even the identity of material lying in the museums is lost. The problem of unpublished excavations is certainly no less serious and regrettable than that of excavations which are both unauthorized and badly conducted; in both cases the results are negative as far as the essential aim of archaeological research is concerned. The excavator pure and simple, however brilliant, is not a true archaeologist. The same is true of the museum curator who, because of a one-sided enthusiasm for his work, allows aesthetic or didactic considerations, or even considerations of personal vanity, to outweigh scientific requirements in arranging and exhibiting collections of antiquities. Moreover, there are scholars working at the desk or in the professorial chair who tend to withdraw into their own critical interests, and to regard with a certain amount of scorn the laborious process of investigation and the tasks of classifying and publishing archaeological material.

Archaeology nowadays suffers considerably from differences of opinion and wasted energy, not only because of these varying degrees of professional bias, but even more severely from the lack of definite programs and of agreement and practical co-ordination among the various activities. The structure of the university schools, the standards of training, and the number and quality of young aspirants to scientific research are seldom intelligently related to the qualifications needed in the professional openings available to these new recruits, who are indispensable and much in demand, but are used in a disorganized and irrational way. This lack of systematic relationship between school and profession is serious in Italy, but even worse in France and other Western European countries, where there is no organized service of antiquities comparable to the Italian one. It does not affect the socialist countries of Eastern Europe, where close coordination is insured through the Academies. A similar problem exists in connection with the need for a general organization of investigations by teams of archaeological experts throughout the world, from the various learned institutions, technical services, universities, etc. The solving of this problem is a matter of extreme urgency.

The progress of studies would clearly benefit enormously, both from the formation of a genuine archaeological organization at an international level (at present barely existing in embryo in such bodies as the International Union of Prehistoric and Protohistoric Sciences, the International Association of Classical Archaeology, etc.), and from an effective co-ordination of researches according to plans agreed on by the scholars and competent authorities of the various countries.

### Archaeology and the present crisis of civilization: toward a new humanism?

It now remains to consider the most important problem of all: the function of archaeology within the framework of historical studies and, more generally, in the main lines of development of modern scientific thought. The vigorous increase in research activity, critical zeal on the part of scholars, official recognition, and universal public interest which characterize this branch of culture in our century would be inexplicable if all this did not correspond to real and contemporary values.

The study of classical antiquity and ancient history has for a long time been dominated almost exclusively by written records, i. e., the Greek and Roman literary sources. The image of the man of antiquity (seen as the model of mankind in the absolute sense, according to the tradition of humanistic ideals) was essentially an ideal and heroic image drawn from the works of the ancient authors. It represented the standard of their times: when all was said and done, Greece and Rome became identified with Plato and Alexander the Great, with Cicero or Caesar. Archaeology itself, in its early stages, was little more than an illustrated commentary on the sources — an attempt to interpret the vase paintings or reliefs in the light of Homer or Virgil, an effort to identify in some statue or other the masterpieces of art described by Pliny or Pausanias. Only with the progress made during the nineteenth century in political, social, juridical, economic, and scientific ideas were the methods and objectives of ancient history directed toward inquiring into the collective phenomena, great and small, of development, the study of institutions, religions, customs, the anonymous factors of the life of society. Thus a contract inscribed on a sheet of papyrus proved to have a historical importance as great as that of a poem by Sappho or a page of Suetonius. At this point, archaeology acquired, all at once, its full value as a means of learning about antiquity: not only through the study of inscriptions, an essential source of history, but also through the direct material evidence of life, religions, taste, products, and techniques. Indeed, in certain sectors such evidence can now be said to be the primary instrument, along with information from the literary sources. It must also be pointed out how much archaeology, in its turn, has contributed in recent years to confirming or re-establishing the truth of the traditions recorded by the ancient authors, often called in question by the hypercritical approach of modern historians, especially those concerning the earliest phases of Greek and Roman history.

We can affirm, therefore, that historical studies in the realm of classical antiquity have nowadays acquired an archaeological facet no less important than the traditional literary one. But when one goes on to consider the reconstruction and study of other past civilizations, such as that of the ancient East before the beginnings of written history, or of prehistory and the past of more distant continents, the value of archaeology as an almost exclusive source of knowledge becomes manifest.

This last observation leads us to consider the problem of the significance of archaeology in the contemporary world, on the wider levels of culture. Hitherto, the formative influences of what we call civilization have been Western and European, centered on a classical and European historical tradition, and an understanding of the origins and growth of those institutions and mental and social attitudes belonging to the world in which we have so far lived (a kind of master plan of history). As we know, however, this world is now changing in a rapid and fundamental manner. As European supremacy declines, we are faced with the problem of a plurality of historical traditions, even of the basic concept of civilization. But, above all, we are witnessing a break-up, with results we cannot foretell, of the framework of a social, cultural, and technical conception of culture thousands of years old, through a crisis possibly without precedent in the whole of past history, or perhaps comparable only, though on a very different scale, to the crisis which some ten thousand years ago initiated the change from the nomadic hunters of remote prehistory to a society of settled communities, the creators of the city and the law. Clearly our world, now universally expanding toward dimensions hitherto unknown, can no longer be satisfied with a history traditionally confined to the origins of our European civilization and the growth of these institutions and structures, which it is itself changing or rejecting. Hence the inexorable and widely observed decline of the old ideas of humanistic culture — glorious, indeed, but now grown too narrow. This new world calls on us to recognize in all the experiences of the past, however distant in time and however widely scattered on the face of the earth, the potentialities of the human spirit in sight of its amazing future prospects of development and conquest.

This world-wide history of humanity can be presented only by archaeology, which alone can help us to cross all the barriers and bridge all the gaps in the individual written traditions, to penetrate far back to the formative processes of human societies, to see their growth as parts of a single picture, to make a detailed factual reconstruction by the collation of innumerable pieces of direct evidence. It will not seem too rash to state that the archaeologist, as a student of the remains of a universal past, may assume in present and future societies the functions previously exercised by the historian, the interpreter of single traditions. The search for man in his origins, in his primordial advances, in the traces, even though anonymous, left by his creative genius, seems a task no less noble and precious than the study of man in the literary documents of his more recent past, and no less worthy of being defined as humanistic. Everything contributes to the belief that archaeology, this young and dynamic expression of the historical sciences, can and should make a valid contribution to the defining of a new form of universal humanism, appropriate to the scientific age.

# BIBLIOGRAPHY

The following references have no scholarly end in view, and make no claim to be complete. They are more in the nature of a list providing additional information on the matters discussed in the text for the educated reader who would like to go into them more thoroughly. For this reason I have included only works on the foundations and methods of archaeology, omitting those dealing specifically with the various ancient civilizations. The bibliography is divided into a general bibliography which is an adequate guide to the material as a whole, and a select bibliography grouped according to the subjects of the different chapters.

GENERAL BIBLIOGRAPHY

ARTZIHOVSKY, A. V. *Osnovy arheologii* (Principles of Archaeology), Moscow, 1954.
CERAM, C. W. *The March of Archaeology*, New York, 1958.
CHILDE, V. G. *Piecing Together the Past,* 4th ed., London, 1952.
CLARK, G. *Archaeology and Society*, New York, 1961.
DAUX, G. *Les Étapes de l'archéologie*, Paris, 1958.
DEONNA, W. *L'archéologie, sa valeur, ses méthodes*, 3 vols., Paris, 1912.
KENYON, K. M. *Beginning in Archaeology*, rev. ed., New York, 1953.
KOEPP, F. *Archäologie*, 3 vols., Leipzig, 1919-20.
LAET, S. J. DE. *Archaeology and Its Problems*, New York, 1957.
LAMING, A. *La Découverte du passé*, Paris, 1952.
LAVAYELLE, J. *Introduction aux études d'archéologie et d'histoire de l'art*, Louvain, 1958.
RIZZO, G. E. in *Storia dell'arte greca*, Turin, 1912, pp. 13-49.
RUMPF, A. *Archäologie*, 2 vols., Berlin, 1953-56.
STARK, C. B. *Systematik und Geschichte der Archäologie der Kunst*, Leipzig, 1880.
WHEELER, R. E. M. *Archaeology from the Earth*, Oxford, 1954.
WOOLLEY, C. L. *Digging up the Past*, Harmondsworth, 1954.


SELECT BIBLIOGRAPHY

A Brief History of Archaeology

BECATTI, G. *Arte e gusto negli scrittori latini*, Florence, 1951.
BEHN, F. *Ausgrabungen und Ausgräber*, Stuttgart, 1955.
——. *Aus europäischer Vorzeit. Grabungsergebnisse*, Stuttgart, 1957.
——. " Archeologiche scoperte " in *Enciclopedia Universale dell'Arte*, I, Rome-Venice, 1958, columns 598-615.
BIEBER, M. *Laocoön. The Influence of the Group since Its Rediscovery,* 2nd ed., Detroit, 1967.
CERAM, C. W. *Gods, Graves and Scholars*, London, 1952.
——. *The World of Archaeology*, London, 1966.

CHANG, KWANG-CHIH. *The Archaeology of Ancient China*, New Haven-London, 1963.

COTTRELL, L. *The Lost Pharaohs. The Romance of Egyptian Archaeology*, New York, 1951.

CUMMING, J. *Revealing India's Past*, London, 1939.

DANIEL, GLYN E. *A Hundred Years of Archaeology*, London, 1950, 2nd ed., 1952.

DEUEL, L. *The Treasure of Time. Firsthand Accounts by Famous Archaeologists of Their Work in the Near East*, Cleveland, 1961.

DIMITROV, D. *Die letzten archäologischen Ausgrabungen in Bulgarien*, Sofia, 1955.

GANN, T. W. *Maya Cities. A Record of Exploration and Adventure in Middle America*, London, 1927.

GRAF, A. *Roma nella memoria e nelle immaginazioni del medio evo*, 2nd ed., Turin, 1923.

GRIMAL, P. *À la recherche de l'Italie antique*, Paris, 1961.

HAUTECOEUR, L. *Rome et la renaissance de l'antiquité à la fin du XVIIIᵉ Siècle*, Paris, 1912.

HENSEL, W., and GIEYSZTOR, A. *Archäologische Forschungen in Polen*, Warsaw, 1958.

HIBBEN, F. C. *Digging up America*, New York, 1960.

HUBNER, P. G. "Le statue di Roma," in *Grundlagen für eine Geschichte der antiken Monumente in der Renaissance*, Leipzig, 1912.

JUSTI, C. *Winckelmann. Sein Leben, seine Werke und seine Zeitgenossen*, Leipzig, 1866-72.

LADENDORF, H. *Antikenstudium und Antikenkopie, Vorarbeiten zu einer Darstellung ihrer Bedeutung in der mittelalterlichen und neueren Zeit*, Berlin, 1953.

LANCIANI, R. *Storia degli scavi di Roma*, 4 vols., Rome, 1902-13.

——. *L'archeologia nel primo cinquantennio della nuova Italia*, Rome, 1912.

LLOYD, S. *Foundations in the Dust. A Story of Mesopotamian Exploration*, Harmondsworth, 1947, 2nd ed., 1955.

MACKENDRICK, P. *The Mute Stones Speak. The Story of Archaeology in Italy*, London, 1960.

——. *The Greek Stones Speak. The Story of Archaeology in the Greek Lands*, New York, 1963.

MALLOWAN, M. E. L. *Twenty-five Years of Mesopotamian Discovery (1932-1956)*, London, 1956.

MICHAELIS, A. *Ein Jahrhundert Kunstarchäologischer Entdeckungen*, Leipzig, 1903, 2nd ed., 1908.

MONGAIT, A. L. *Arheologija SSSR*, Moscow, n.d.

MOSCATI, S. *Scoprendo l'antico Oriente*, Bari, 1962.

OPPELN-BRONIKOWSKI, F. VON. *Archäologische Entdeckungen im 20. Jahrhundert*, Berlin, 1930.

PARROT, A. *Discovering Buried Worlds*, New York, 1955.

PATON, J. M. *Chapters on Mediaeval and Renaissance Visitors to Greek Lands*, Princeton, 1951.

SALIS, A. VON. *Antike und Renaissance. Über Nachleben und Weiterwirken der alten in der neueren Kunst*, Erlenbach-Zurich, 1947.

SCHEFOLD, K. (ed). *Fasti Archeologici*, Florence, from 1946.

——. *Orient, Hellas und Rom in der archäologischen Forschung seit 1939*, Bern, 1949.

——. *Neue deutsche Ausgrabungen im Mittelmeergebiet und im Vorderen Orient*, Berlin, 1959.

SCHULTEN, A. *Cincuenticinco años de investigacion en España*, Reus, 1953.

——. *Neue Ausgrabungen in Deutschland*, Berlin, 1958.

WACE, A. J. B. "The Greeks and Romans as Archaeologists," *Bulletin de la Société Royale d'Archéologie d'Alexandrie*, XXXVIII (1949), pp. 21-35.

WEBER, S. H. *Voyages and Travels in Greece, the Near East and Adjacent Regions Made Previous to the Year 1801*, Princeton, 1953.

Archaeology for "Non-professional" Motives

ALBIZZATI, C. "Varia de Centuripis," *Athenaeum*, XXXVI (1948), pp. 237 *ff.*

BOTHMER, D. VON, and NOBLE, J. V. *An Inquiry into the Forgery of the Etruscan Terracotta Warriors in the Metropolitan Museum of Art (Metropolitan Museum Papers, 11)*, New York, 1961.

CAGIANO DE AZEVEDO, M. "Falsi settecenteschi di pitture antiche," *Bollettino dell'Istituto Centrale del Restauro*, I (1950), pp. 41-43.

CANTONE, A. C. *Ordinamento dell'Amministrazione delle Antichità e Belle Arti*, Rome, 1963.

COLE, S. *Faux crânes et faux tableaux*, Paris, 1958,

COURAJOD, L. *L'imitation et la contrefaçon des objets d'art antique*, Paris, 1887.

DESROCHES-NOBLECOURT, C. *Temples de Nubie. Des trésors menacés*, Paris, 1961.

GRISOLIA, M. *International Protection of Works of Art and Historic Monuments*, Department of State, Washington, D.C., 1949.

——. *La tutela delle cose d'arte*, 1952.

——. "Difendiamo il patrimonio artistico," *Ulisse*, XI (1957), fasc. 27.

——. "Symposium on Salvage," *Archaeology*, 14 (1961), no. 4.

ISNARD, G. *Faux et imitations dans l'art*, Paris, 1959.

LAVACHERY, H., and NOBLECOURT, A. *Les techniques de protection des biens culturels en cas de conflit armé*, Paris, 1954.

LERICI, C. M. *Italia sepolta*, Milan, 1962.

——. *La protezione del patrimonio artistico nazionale dalle offese della guerra aerea*, Florence, 1942.

SALMON, P. *De la collection au musée*, Brussels, 1958.

TAYLOR, F. H. *The Taste of Angels. A History of Collecting from Rameses to Napoleon*, Boston, 1948.

TURKEL, S. *Prähistorische Fälschungen. Eine Rundfrage*, Graz, 1927.

VAYSON DE PRADENNE, A. *L'affaire de Glozel*, Paris, 1928.

——. *Les fraudes en archéologie préhistorique*, Paris, 1932.

WEINER, J. S. *The Piltdown Forgery*, New York, 1955.

The Great Archaeological Themes

ALLEGRO, J. M. *The Dead Sea Scrolls*, Harmondsworth, 1956.

BEHN, F. *Vor und Frühgeschichte, Grundlagen, Aufgaben, Methode*, Wiesbaden, 1948.

BERENSON, B. *L'Arco di Costantino o della decadenza della forma*, Florence, 1952.

BIASUTTI, R. *Le razze e i popoli della terra*, 3rd ed., Turin, 1953-57.

BIBBY, G. *The Testimony of the Spade*, New York, 1956.

BOSSERT, H. T., and ZSCHEITZSCHMANN, W. *Hellas und Rom. Die Kultur der Antike in Bildern*, Berlin, 1936.

CABROL, F., and LECLERCQ, E. *Dictionnaire d'archéologie chrétienne et de liturgie*, Paris, 1903.

CHADWICK, J. *The Decipherment of Linear B*, 2nd ed., New York, 1960.

DAREMBERG, C., and SAGLIO, E. *Dictionnaire des antiquités grecques et romaines*, Paris, 1887-1916.

DOBLHOFER, E. *Voices in Stone. The Decipherment of Ancient Scripts and Writings*, New York, 1961.

EBERT, M. *Real-lexikon der Vorgeschichte*, Berlin, 1924-32.

*Enciclopedia dell'arte antica classica e orientale*, Rome, from 1958.

*Encyclopedia of World Art*, New York, from 1959.

FRIEDRICH, J. *Entzifferung verschollener Schriften und Sprachen*, Berlin-Gottingen-Heidelberg, 1954.

GUARDUCCI, M. *La tomba di Pietro*, Rome, 1959.

HEBERER, G., KURTH, G., and SCHWIDETZKY-ROESSING, I. *Anthropologie*, Frankfort, 1959.

"In memoria di Luigi Lanza," *Studi Etruschi*, XXIX (1961), pp. i-xli.

KIRSCHBAUM, E. *The Tombs of St. Peter and St. Paul*, New York, 1959.

MAIURI, A. *Pompei ed Ercolano*, Padua, 1950.

——. *Pompeiana*, Naples, 1950.

MENGHIN, O. *Weltgeschichte der Steinzeit*, Vienna, 1931.

MONTANDON, G. *Traité d'ethnologie culturelle*, Paris, 1934.

MOORE, R. *Menschen, Zeiten und Fossilien. Roman der Anthropologie*, Reinbeck bei Hamburg, 1951.

MÜLLER, SOPHUS. *Urgeschichte Europas. Grundzüge einer prähistorischen Archäologie*, Strasbourg, 1905.

RICCIOTTI, G. *La Bibbia e le scoperte moderne*, Florence, 1957.

RIEGL, A. *Spätrömische Kunstindustrie*, Vienna, 1901, 2nd. ed., 1927.

RUYSSCHARERT, J. "Recherches et études autour de la Confession de la Basilique Vaticane (1940-1958). État de la question et bibliographie," in *Triplice omaggio a S. S. Pio XII*, II, Città del Vaticano, 1958, pp. 33-47.

VAUX, R. DE. *L'archéologie et les manuscrits de la Mer Morte,* London, 1961.

WILLEY, G. R., and PHILLIPS, P. *Method and Theory in American Archaeology,* Chicago, 1958.

WRIGHT, G. E. *Biblical Archaeology,* Philadelphia, 1957.


Archaeology in Action

AITKEN, M. J. *Physics and Archaeology,* New York, 1961.

ANDRAE, W. *Babylon, die versunkene Weltstadt und ihr Ausgraber Robert Koldewey,* Berlin, 1952.

——. *Lebenserinnerungen eines Ausgrabers,* Berlin, 1961.

ATKINSON, R. C. *Field Archaeology,* London, 1946, 2nd ed., 1953.

AVDUSIN, D. A. *Arheologiceskie razvedki i raskopti* (Archaeological research and excavation), Moscow, 1959.

BASS, G. F. *Archaeology Under Water,* London, 1966.

BERNARDINI, M. *Scopi pratici dell'archeologia e ordinamento dei musei,* Bari, 1955.

BORHEGYI, SUZANNE DE. *Ships, Shoals and Amphoras,* New York, 1961.

BRADFORD, J. *Ancient Landscapes. Studies in Field Archaeology,* London, 1957.

BRAIDWOOD, R. J. *Archaeologists and What They Do,* New York, 1960.

BROTHWELL, D. R. *Digging up Bones. The Excavation, Treatment and Study of Human Skeletal Remains,* London, 1963.

—— and HIGGS, E. (eds.) *Science in Archaeology,* London, 1963.

CAGIANO DE AZEVEDO, M. *Il gusto nel restauro delle opere d'arte antiche,* Rome, 1948.

——. *Museen und Museumskunde im 20. Jahrhundert,* Zurich, 1952.

——. "Nouvelles tendances de la présentation dans les musées archéologiques," in *Museum,* 1953, pp. 1-69.

CHEVALIER, E. *Bibliographie des applications archéologiques de la photographie aérienne,* Milan, 1957.

CRAWFORD, O. G. S. *Archaeology in the Field,* London, 1953, 2nd ed., 1960.

DIOLÉ, P. *Four Thousand Years Under the Sea,* London, 1954.

——. *Atti del II Congresso Internazionale di Archeologia Sottomarina,* Albenga, 1958, Bordighera, 1961.

DUGRACQ, A. *La science à la conquête du passé,* Paris, 1955.

DUMAS, F. *Deep Water Archaeology,* London, 1962.

DU MESNIL DU BUISSON, ROBERT, COMTE. *La technique des fouilles archéologiques,* Paris, 1934.

FORBES, E. J. *Metallurgy in Antiquity. A Notebook for Archaeologists and Technologists,* Leiden, 1950.

FRANZEN, A. *The Warship Vasa. Deep Diving and Marine Archaeology in Stockholm,* 2nd ed., Stockholm, 1960.

HEIZER, R. F., and COOK, S. C. *The Application of Quantitative Methods in Archaeology,* Chicago, 1960.

HOERMANN, H. *Methodik der Denkmalpflege,* Munich, 1938.

LAMBOGLIA, N., and BENOIT, F. *Scavi sottomarini in Liguria e in Provence,* Bordighera, 1953.

LERICI, G. M. *Alla scoperta delle civiltà sepolte. I nuovi metodi di prospezione archeologica,* Milan, 1960.

LEROI-GOURHAN, A. *Les fouilles préhistoriques. Technique et méthodes,* Paris, 1960.

LIBBY, W. F. *Radiocarbon Dating,* 2nd ed., Chicago, 1955.

LOW, T. L. *The Museum as a Social Instrument,* New York, 1942.

MAIURI, A. *Vita d'archeologo. Cronache dell'archeologia napoletana,* Naples, 1958.

OLDEBERG, A. *Metalltechnik under forhistorik,* 2 vols., Lund, 1942-43.

PESCHECK, C. *Lehrbuch der Urgeschichtsforschung,* Weende-Göttingen, 1950.

PLENDERLEITH, H. J. *The Conservation of Antiquities and Works of Art. Treatment, Repair, and Restoration,* New York, 1956.

POOLE, L. and G. *One Passion, Two Loves: The Story of Heinrich and Sophia Schliemann, Discoverers of Troy,* New York, 1966.

RATHGEN, F. *Die Konservierung von Altertumsfunden,* 3 vols., Leipzig, 1926.

ROGHI, G. *L'archeologo*, Florence, 1961.

RUDOLFF-HILLE, G. *Hilfsbuch der Museumsarbeit*, Dresden, 1953.

SALMANG, H. *Die physikalischen und chemischen Grundlagen der Keramik*, 2nd ed., Berlin, 1951.

SCHLIEMANN, H. *Selbstbiographie*, 3rd ed., Leipzig, 1939.

——. *Briefwechsel*, Berlin, 1953.

SHEPARD, A. O. *Ceramics for the Archaeologists*, Washington, D.C., 1957.

SMITH, R. *Bibliography of Museums and Museum Work*, Washington, D.C., 1928.

UCCELLI, G. *Le navi di Nemi*, Rome, 1940.

ZEUNER, F. E. *Dating the Past*, London, 1946, 4th ed., 1958.

ZUCHNER, W. *Über die Abbildung*, Berlin, 1959.

# INDEX

All numbers refer to pages. Those printed in *italic type* refer to the pages on which captions appear, with pages for colorplate captions further indicated by an asterisk (*25**)

347

The purpose of the table on the following page is to offer the reader, at a glance and in graphic form, a review of the civilizations dealt with in the text, and, albeit in very general terms, to show their relationship to one another, their geographical distribution and their duration. The scope of the table is purely practical and indicative and it does not attempt an historical synthesis which would be impossible in our present state of knowledge, and in any case out of place at the end of a volume not concerned with the systematic study of ancient civilizations. Even the dates, especially in the more remote periods, must be accepted with every reserve.

In order to simplify the reading of the table I have divided the various cultures into eleven groups. This grouping is naturally a conventional device but it does correspond roughly to the classifications current among students of prehistory, archaeology and ancient history and therefore does not require special clarification. The limits of the table must of necessity remain undetermined owing to the nature of archaeological research beyond the confines of the "ancient world" (see pages 194-221 of the text), and this applies especially to Medieval Europe, India and the Far East.

The table is followed by an index by subject matter where the reader is referred to the parts of the text dealing with specific subjects and more especially to the relevant illustrations and colorplates. The reader who, for example, wishes to have an idea of the aspects of ancient Egyptian civilization discussed, and to know what Egyptian monuments and works of art are included among the illustrations, will find these indications under the heading *Near Eastern Cultures – Egypt.* In the index I have grouped together *Euro-Asiatic Cultures* and *Indo-European Invasions* which, for graphic simplification, are separated in the table but are in fact linked geographically north of the Near and Middle Eastern regions and in the Mediterranean. Under this heading I have placed together all the protohistoric cultures of the Metal Age and the Bronze and Iron Ages, which spread through the two continents outside the areas of development of the great cultures of South West Asia, the Mediterranean and China.

The last part of the index is concerned with the spread of archaeological knowledge in medieval and modern times and to the influence of the ancient world on art, culture and taste throughout history.

# CHIEF CIVILIZATIONS OF ARCHAEOLOGICAL INTEREST

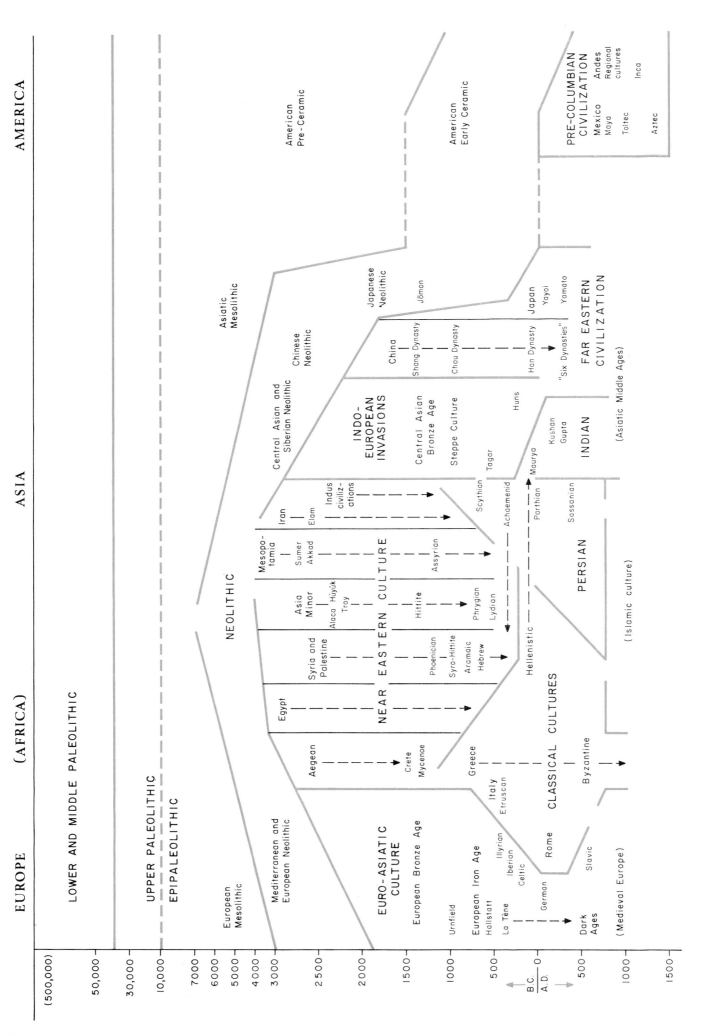

Nouveau, *123*; the Mausoleum of Ataturk in Ankara (1940), *125*; government offices in Oslo with runic decoration, *124*; Central Library of the University of Mexico (1951-53), *125*; *Son et Lumière* in the Roman Forum, *96*; classical inspiration in contemporary art: Picasso, *131*; de Chirico, *131*; Dali, *131*; Nicholson, *131*.

Museology: the garden-museum of Jacopo Galli (from a drawing by M. van Heemskerck 1532-36), *74*; the courtyard of the Palazzo Valle-Capranica in Rome (engraving by H. Cock, 1553), *74*; *Un Cabinet d'Amateur de Tableaux* (painting by F. Francken the Younger), *75*; the Rotunda of the Museo Pio Clementino in the Vatican (end of the eighteenth century), *300*; Villa Borghese in Rome (early nineteenth century), *77*; the dome of Sir John Soane's Museum in London (early nineteenth century), *77*; transfer of the Bourbon collections to Naples in 1822 (contemporary engraving), *76*; the Loggia dei Lanzi in Florence, *75*; the Louvre stairway with the *Victory of Samothrace*, *301*; the Bardo Museum in Tunis (1888), *302*; the Egyptian Museum in Cairo (1895-1900), *303**; the gallery of casts in the Istituto di Archeologia at the University of Rome, *312*; the Oslo Museum, *307*; the Gela Museum in Sicily (1958), *305*.

LOCALITIES OF ARCHAEOLOGICAL INTEREST IN THE ANCIENT WORLD

Taxila
Harappa
Indus River
Begram
Balkh
Mohenjo Daro
Toprak Kale
Persepolis
Susa
Nineveh
Ziwiyeh
Assur
Nemrut Dağ
Tell Halaf
Mari
Ctesiphon
Babylon
Uruk
Ur
Dura Europos
Ugarit
Antioch
Baalbek
Jericho
Jerusalem
Dead Sea
Sidon
Tyre
Rosetta
Alexandria
Memphis
Tell-el-Amarna
Thebes
Abu Simbel
Novgorod
Kerch
Olbia
Cucuteni
Istria
Nagyszentmiklos
Alaca Hüyük
Boghazköy
Gordion
Troy
Pergamon
Sardis
Çatal Hüyük
Ephesus
Miletus
Karatepe
CYPRUS
RHODES
Olynthus
Constantinople
Pella
Athens
Delphi
Corinth
Knossos
CRETE
Phaistos
Mycenae
Pylos
Cyrene
Leptis Magna
Poznan
Cologne
Trier
Heuneburg
Hallstatt
Virunum
Vix
Lyons
Aquileia
Ravenna
Spina
Arezzo
Perugia
Vulci
Rome
Palestrina
Tarquinia
Cerveteri
Naples
Herculaneum
Pompeii
Paestum
Tarentum
Piazza Armerina
Olympia
Syracuse
Gela
Palermo
MALTA
Stonehenge
Maintenon
Roufignac
Arles
Marseilles
Albenga
Hippo Regius
Carthage
Mahdia
Timgad
Ibiza
BALEARIC ISLES
Barumini
Tarragona
Altamira
Numantia
Mérida
Cádiz
Lixus
Volubilis

0    300
miles